TAKE IT BY FORCE!

Violent Prayers for Deliverance, Healing, and Financial Breakthrough

DANIEL C. OKPARA

Includes:

A 3-Day Fasting and Prayers Plan for Deliverance, Healing, and Breakthrough

Copyright © August 2016 by Daniel C. Okpara.

All Rights Reserved. Contents of this book may not be reproduced in any way or by any means without written consent of the publisher, with the exception of brief excerpts in critical reviews and articles.

Published By:

Better Life Media.

BETTER LIFE WORLD OUTREACH CENTER.

Website: www.BetterLifeWorld.org

Email: info@betterlifeworld.org

Any scripture quotation in this book is taken from the King James Version or New International Version, except where stated. Used by permission.

All texts, calls, letters, testimonies, and inquiries are welcome.

CONTENTS

FREE BONUS …6

How to Navigate Through This Book…7

Introduction…10

PART 1: HOW VIOLENT PRAYERS WORK…17

Chapter 1: What is Violent Prayers?…18

Chapter 2: Effects of Praying Violent Prayers…35

Chapter 3: When You Need to Pray Violent Prayers and Minister Deliverance to Yourself or Home…49

Chapter 4: How to Minister Deliverance to Yourself or to Someone Else…72

PART 2: 3 DAYS FASTING AND PRAYERS GUIDE FOR DELIVERANCE, HEALING AND BREAKTHROUGH…82

Chapter 5: Instructions for Praying…83

Chapter 6: Day 1: Prayers of Confession, Forgiveness, Rededication, Holy Spirit Empowerment, and Deliverance from Bad Habits and Addictions…84

Chapter 7: Day 2: Prayers to Destroy Curses from Family Lineage, and Enforce Your Personal Deliverance from Demonic Attacks and Oppressions…96

Chapter 8: Day 3: Prayers Against Self Imposed Curses, Challenges, Spiritual Attacks. and Ministering to Yourself...109

Chapter 9: Bring to God an Offering of Midnight Praise...123

PART 3: VIOLENT PRAYERS FOR HEALING, BUSINESS AND FINANCIAL BREAKTHROUGH, AND FREEDOM FROM DEPRESSION AND HEALING OF ANGUISH (INNER HURTS)...127

Chapter 10: 30 Violent Prayers for Healing...128

Chapter 11: Violent Prayers for Business and Financial Breakthrough...139

Chapter 12: 20 Powerful Prayers for Healing of Inner Wounds, Comfort and Freedom from Depression...159

Chapter 13: 5 Ways to Maintain Your Victory, Healing and Deliverance...168

Other Books by the Same Author...174

Get in Touch...176

About the Author...177

NOTES...178

FREE BONUS ...

Download These 4 Powerful Books Today for FREE... And Take Your Relationship With God to a New Level.

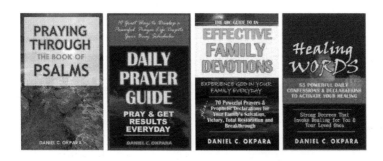

Go Here to Download

www.betterlifeworld.org/grow

How to Navigate Through This Book

This book is divided into three parts, and contains about 13 chapters. Part one includes four chapters and discusses what violent prayers are all about. We answer some great questions all geared at motivating you to arise and declare your freedom in Christ Jesus.

In chapter one, for example, I explain that contrary to your first impression on sighting the term "VIOLENT PRAYERS," it is not shouting in prayers. It is not disturbing the neighborhood; it's a different kind of prayer strategy that invokes God's power and sends the works of the devil packing.

In chapter 2, I show you a few men and women who prayed violently in the Bible and the results they obtained. My goal is to encourage you to pray violently from today.

Then in chapter 3, we discuss extensively when a child

of God needs to pray violent prayers. Chapter 3 is very detailed and also shows you signs of demonic attacks in your life and family. Chapter 3 should be a reference manual for diagnosing spiritual problems and proposing solutions.

In chapter 4, I show you steps to minister deliverance to yourself, family or someone else. Those are steps involved in the process of violent prayers.

Then enter PART 2

The part two contains carefully selected violent Prayers for Healing, Business and Financial Breakthrough, Freedom from Depression and Healing of Anguish (Inner Hurts).

The only difference between Part 3 and Part 4 is that you can take the prayers in Part 4 and apply them anytime, with or without fasting, while Part 3 assumes that you will be fasting and praying for three days and thus outlines the prayers in day by day format.

However you decide to use this book and the prayers in it, what I'm certain about is that the power of God will flow through to you and cause you to experience a powerful touch that will change your life for the better.

"After going through the prayers and declarations in this book for 3 days, all the evil harassments and threats in your life and family will end."

Introduction

The prayers in this book are carefully put together to empower anyone going through demonic oppression, spiritual attacks, illnesses, financial hardship or any anguish at the moment to obtain freedom and breakthrough.

The prayers in this book will bow any difficulty in your life. They will enable you to have great revelations that will give you direction, and all closed doors against you will open.

After going through the prayers and declarations in this book for 3 days, all the evil harassments and threats in your life and family will end. You will receive physical healing if you are sick in the body. If you are praying for the fruit of the womb, you'll conceive. If your case is marriage disappointment, it will be settled.

Before you go forward, here's what I want you to do…

1. MAKE A LIST.

Before you go into prayer with this book, sit down first. Take a sheet of paper and list out all the wrong things happening in your life at the moment that needs to be settled. Praying with clarity is important.

Don't worry if there are so many things you don't like at the moment happening in your life that needs to be settled as quickly as possible. Just list them out. Here's what I mean:

WRONG THINGS I DON'T WANT	THINGS I WANT
Depression- I'm depressed	Peace and Joy – I want peace, joy and comfort.
Fights in my home	I want peace and love to be restored
Financial difficulties- I can't meet my financial obligations right now.	Financial breakthrough – I need a breakthrough financially. I need a new job. I need a new business idea, etc.
Nightmares – I'm having nightmares, and I hear voices of suicide.	I want to have dreams from the LORD and hear voices of life and Hope…
I'm sick of…….	I need instant healing and freedom from this…………

Now you get what I mean. We need to be specific about your needs. We need to list out the negative things that are happening and the positive expectations to replace them.

Getting clarity before embarking on a prayer session, such as the kind of prayer session recommended in this book is very important.

Blind Bartimeus cried and got through to Jesus; while standing before him, even though Jesus could see that he was blind, He still asked him, "What do you want me to do for you?"

God wants us to be clear on things we are praying about.

2. ASSURANCE.

Like I said, you will receive answers to your prayers. That is the conviction that the Spirit of God has asked me to give you. Several months from today, you will go back to your list and wonder in awe what the LORD has done.

I'm in agreement with you all through the prayers in this book. The God of heaven, our loving Father, will touch your life and give you a great testimony.

3. WHY 3 DAYS FASTING?

Fasting is a key to the impossible. If you go through the Bible, you will notice that many difficult problems and situations were addressed by 'FASTED' PRAYER.

I describe fasting as ***fastens*** your prayer. Jesus said that some problems can only be fixed by prayer and fasting (Matthew 17:21).

There are different kinds of fasting. However, that is not the focus of this book. Whatever type of fasting you can do, that is okay. I usually encourage people to drink water when they are fasting. If you can skip dinner to pray the prayers in this book efficiently in the night, that's better.

Skipping dinner is a fast that Apostle J.N.J of Apostolic Research Institute taught me. He skipped dinner for six months and spent all nights seeking the LORD in prayers over some severe issues of direction in ministry. And the LORD came through to him in an obvious way, took away his confusion and led him through one of the worst crisis times of his life.

Skipping dinner fast is especially useful as it helps you to go about your business in the day and then seek the LORD for one hour or more in the nights.

We are in spiritual warfare. There are enemies bent on frustrating your life and making sure you go through pain and shame. But as we humble ourselves before the

LORD, we receive strength and direction to resist these coordinated forces of wickedness and obtain God's blessings designed for our lives.

Fasting increases the power of prayer several times over. This book recommends and assumes that you will fast for three days and go through the prayer sessions.

Whichever kind of fasting you decide to do, whether it is 6-10am, 6-12:00 noon, 6PM-6AM, that's okay. Whether it's the skipping dinner fasting that you choose to do, that's okay and great. What is important is that you realize the need to humble yourself before the LORD and pray. The Bible says:

> *"Is not this the kind of fasting I have chosen: to loose the chains of injustice and untie the cords of the yoke, to set the oppressed free and break every yoke? –* **Isaiah 58:6**

> *While they were worshiping the Lord in fasting, the Holy Spirit said,* **"Separate for me Barnabas and Saul for the work to which I have**

> ***called them."** So after they had fasted and prayed, they placed their hands on them and sent them off. –*
> ***Acts 13:2-3***

In this 3 days fasting and violent prayers, the chains of injustice against your life and family will be destroyed. The yoke of heaviness in your life or any member of your family will be loosed; you and your family members will be set free from the oppression of the devil; and the Holy Spirit will speak and give you direction.

PART 1:

How Violent Prayers Work

Chapter 1: What is Violent Prayers?

Let me tell you what violent prayer is and why you need to pray violent prayers. Jesus said:

> *"And from the days of John the Baptist until now the kingdom of heaven suffereth violence, and the violent take it by force."* – **Matthew 11:12 (KJV)**

In this text, Jesus was talking about John the Baptist, His forerunner. He tells us how John the Baptist is the greatest of all men born before him, and how, even now, the lowest in the kingdom would become greater than him.

He then says that the kingdom of God advances only with violence and it's only the violent that takes it by force.

Okay, this is not talking about Jihad. It's not talking about killing people and forcing them to convert to your faith. But it's talking about something we need to pay attention to.

You see, John the Baptist was the one who confessed to the whole world that Jesus was the Christ. But somehow, he fell out with the government of his day and was arrested and put in prison. Right in prison, apparently worried how Jesus did not come and set him free with some miraculous demonstration, he began to doubt if Jesus was the savior as he had publicly proclaimed before the world. He now sent his disciples to ask Jesus if He was indeed the Christ.

Touched by that question, Jesus began to explain to the people about who John the Baptist was and in the process made that statement.

Simply put, Jesus was saying that the whole powers of heaven were at the disposal of John the Baptist. But instead of placing a demand on heaven and saying, "hey, I'm out of this place right now. Let fire from heaven answer for me now."

Instead of saying, "Jesus, Son of David, arise and come to my rescue."

Instead of saying, "LORD, I refuse to die another man's death."

He sent emissaries to Jesus to ask, "Bro, I hope I didn't make a mistake? Are you the Christ?"

What then happened?

John the Baptist was later killed like a commoner. His head was severed and offered on a platter at the request of a dancer.

What a tragedy!

Yes, he went to heaven. But I don't think that was how he was destined to go. Remember that John the Baptist possessed the same Spirit that Elijah possessed. Can you imagine what Elijah would have done to those people?

My point is this: **God did not save us as Christians, so we can just go to heaven only. He saved us so we can live a victorious life here on earth before coming to heaven.** He saved us and gave us the power to deal with the devil and his oppositions and command whatever rises to harass our redemption to bow and leave.

If you don't rise up and use your authority, the devil and his demons will buffet you like an ordinary servant and cause you unnecessary pains. He will afflict your mind and create sickness in your body, and leave you wondering what's happening. He will make you think that you are just a powerless fellow and that you can do nothing but only accept your situation.

But that's a lie.

You are not meant to be harassed and afflicted.

"Anything contrary to peace that passes all understanding; anything contrary to abundant life; anything contrary to sound mind and healthy body; anything contrary to moving from strength to strength, from one level to another higher level; anything contrary to a healthy and loving family; anything contrary to God's promises is not your portion."

When they raise their ugly heads, you must return fire. When you sense demonic attacks, you must return fire.

You cannot beg the devil. He doesn't understand begging.

The only language the devil understands is FIRE. The only language he listens to is violent prayers.

SO WHAT IS VIOLENT PRAYERS?

First, violent prayers are not making noise in your neighborhood and disturbing everyone so that they will know you are praying.

It's more than that.

Where necessary, you may pray out loud, provided that is not going to be an inconvenience to others.

But violent prayers are more than shouting in prayer. It involves 3 elements:

1: THOUGHT PROCESS

Violent prayers are a mindset. It's the mindset that says,

> "Enough is enough. I'm going to get my deliverance. It's time to get my breakthrough. Whatever is standing between me and my open doors must

> *be destroyed, and I must enter into my open doors in Jesus' name.*
>
> *"I cannot continue like this.*
>
> *"LORD Jesus, I know You died for me to have peace of mind, to be healthy and prosper. So whatever is contrary to Your promises in my life must leave my life. And they must go now."*

The first stage of violent prayers refuses to accept anything contrary to God's promises in your life. For instance, if you are having nightmares every day, and this is now causing you to be afraid, you have to say, "Okay, enough! This nonsense needs to stop"

If you're addicted to pornography, alcohols, lust and other strongholds, you'll say, **"LORD, I'm going to end this nonsense, and I must do it right away. Devil, I'm done. Enough"**

If you're always getting sickly, you'll say, "LORD, this isn't supposed to be so. I'm not going to accept this pain. This cancer is not of You. I'm going to get healed and have my peace."

That mindset is the first stage of violent prayers.

2: PUSH

PUSH stands for – Pray Until Something Happens.

All bible men and women who ever got answers to their prayers PUSHED – They prayed Until Something Happened. They didn't pray a few times and then started doubting and blaming the ALMIGHTY GOD and asking, "Does God answer prayers? Are you sure I'm not gonna die like this"

Of course, God answers prayers. I am not saying this in His defense. But I know that God answers prayers. We only need to learn how to PUSH. We need to learn how the spirit world works.

For example, if you need deliverance from demonic attacks and breakthrough, you have to PUSH. Without learning how to PUSH, you may never see answers to your prayers.

WHO NEEDS TO PUSH?

Everyone who wants to see answers to their prayers. YOU. Without PUSHING, the devil will keep contending with the Angels of God bringing our miracles and answers and delaying them unnecessarily. That is how the spirit world works.

When you kneel down to pray and ask God for anything, our loving Father quickly dispatches angels to go and bring you what you are praying about. But the devil can waylay these angels in the spirit world and engage them. In the physical realm, this now causes unnecessary delays. But as we continue to PUSH, our prayers continue to resist these evil spirits and their father, the devil, until they give up and we get our answers.

Read this scripture below and tell me what you think:

> *7 Then war broke out in heaven. Michael and his angels fought against the dragon, and the dragon and his angels fought back. 8 But he was not strong enough, and they lost their place in heaven.*
>
> *9 The great dragon was hurled down— that ancient serpent called the devil, or Satan, who leads the whole world*

> *astray. He was hurled to the earth, and his angels with him -* **Revelation 12:7-9**

Isn't that interesting? If the devil could put up a fight in heaven, trying to overthrow the ALMIGHTY GOD himself, don't think he'll not put up a fight against your prayers and wellbeing.

In fact, verse 12 of that same scripture captures the mindset of the devil after he was cast down.

> *"Therefore rejoice you heavens and you who dwell in them! But woe to the earth and the sea, because the devil has gone down to you! He is filled with fury because he knows that his time is short."*

The devil is fighting with all his strength because he knows that his time is short. He will do everything he can to stop your prayers from being answered because he knows that when you get answers to your prayers, your faith will increase and your service and dedication to God will become great. So he will put up all manner of resistance between the time you prayed and when the answer comes.

That gap between when you prayed and when the answer comes is the devil's play time. He will try to accuse you and say, *"hey, don't you know you are a sinner. You did this the other day. You cursed the other day, so you aren't getting anything."*

He will inspire men who will become obstacles to your expectation, people who will put a lot of stumbling blocks in your ways. If you don't know how to PUSH, your prayers will then be unnecessarily delayed.

Apostle Paul said:

> *For a great door and effectual is opened unto me, and there are many adversaries -* **1 Corinthians 16:9**

Many great doors for ministry were opened for him, but he had a lot of opponents to contend. That's more like saying, *"I can see a great opening and opportunities ahead, but I just can't get in to utilize them, because adversaries are opposing me and trying to scheme me out."*

The NET Bible puts that scripture this way: **"because a**

door of great opportunity stands wide open for me, but there are many opponents."

He prayed for open doors. He could see doors open before him. But opponents and adversaries won't just let him.

This is the same kind of game the enemy is playing with us Christians. When we pray, God answers. But the opposition raises adversaries, spiritual and physical stumbling blocks so that we don't get into the opportunities ahead of us.

But today, like Apostle Paul and other great saints of God, we'll start pushing back the forces of darkness and taking back what belongs to us with violent prayers.

3: AUTHORITATIVE PRAYING:

Violent, intense praying is not just any praying. In violent prayer, you pray with authority. You command, you don't beg. Let me give you an example.

> [46] *Then they came to Jericho. As Jesus and his disciples, together with a large crowd, were leaving the city, a blind man, Bartimaeus (which means "son of Timaeus"), was sitting by the roadside*

begging. ⁴⁷ When he heard that it was Jesus of Nazareth, he began to shout, "Jesus, Son of David, have mercy on me!"

⁴⁸ Many rebuked him and told him to be quiet, but he shouted all the more, "Son of David, have mercy on me!"

⁴⁹ Jesus stopped and said, **"Call him."**

So they called to the blind man, "Cheer up! On your feet! He's calling you." ⁵⁰ Throwing his cloak aside, he jumped to his feet and came to Jesus.

⁵¹ "What do you want me to do for you?" Jesus asked him.

The blind man said, "Rabbi, I want to see."

⁵² **"Go,"** said Jesus, **"your faith has healed you."** Immediately he received his sight and followed Jesus along the road. – **Mark 10:46-52**

That's a combination of the three aspects of violent prayers. His mind was made up on getting healed, and he pushed through the crowd authoritatively

When he prayed first – "Son of David, have mercy on me....."

Jesus didn't stop.

The multitudes created a distance between him and the Savior. He needed to do something about the multitudes. He needed to get through them.

Same way, when we pray, God hears and answers our prayers, but there's a distance that exists between the spirit world and our world. We need to press through that gap and ensure that the multitudes there don't stop us from receiving what we have prayed for.

FAST FOOD PRAYING.

I've learned that prayers seldom work like a "fast food."

You know "fast food." You just check into a restaurant, go through the menu, place an order, and in a flash, the food is ready. And "zam"- you are out.

"Fast food!

Many Christians these days are "Fast food" kind of Christians.

We pray, *"LORD, Please get me healed, in Jesus name. Thank YOU, LORD."*

And if it doesn't happen immediately we say, *"Well, looks like I'm gonna die after all."*

Friend, it's not so.

When you pray, you need to press your way through the crowd. You need to push your way out of the noise. You need to outshout the sounds and voices of the devil trying to get you stuck with your unfavorable condition.

Bartimeus was like,

"Hey, I've got to do everything to get this guy's attention today. I'm done begging. It's time for me to have my deliverance and be a normal fellow."

When people told him to shut up, he cried louder. When they told him to calm down and stop disturbing them, he cried the more.

The Bible says:

> *"Many rebuked him and told him to be quiet, but he shouted all the more, "Son of David, have mercy on me!" - v48*

Imagine that.

For some of us, that first time we pray and Jesus seemed not to take notice was enough to resign and say, *"okay, how do I manage this situation."*

But Bartimaeus won't take any of that. When people rebuked him, he fought back. He shouted the more.

The guy was done begging. *"If this Jesus did all the miracles I have heard before now, then I must get Him to talk to me. You guys can't stop me."*

That was his mindset.

That's violent prayer.

You make up your mind to be free. You ain't taking that pain no more. Then you pray. If the answer doesn't come immediately, you pray some more.

When the devil brings up people to shut you up and tell you it's okay to suffer pain and be oppressed, and tell you to find a way to cope; you say to the devil, no. You thank the people for their opinions and suggestions, but then you pray some more. And you don't stop until the power of God is made manifest in your life.

Violent prayer is not some, *"LORD, please I need to have my peace of mind, please help me, LORD."*

No.

You say,

> *"LORD Jesus, I thank You for the sacrifice YOU made for me to have salvation, deliverance, healing, and prosperity. It is not Your will for me to be troubled and attacked by the devil. So I'm not going to accept this condition. Whatever is responsible for this pain I'm going through, must leave, in Jesus' name.*

And you keep **Praying Until Something Happens**...until you have some peace within you that it's done.

That's violent prayers

THE DEVIL IS FIGHTING HARD TO STOP YOU

This is not a mere religious statement. There is a spiritual war going on against your life. Principalities and powers have vowed never to allow you receive your healing, deliverance, and breakthrough. You've prayed many times and consulted many ministers who also prayed. But it still looks like the same story.

Beloved, it's because there is a spiritual resistance going on against your life. You need to start pushing back the forces of darkness. You need to arise and say, enough is enough. You need to say,

> "No way. I'm going to get my healing, deliverance, and breakthrough. I'm going to see my kids saved and serving the LORD. I'm going to get out of this addiction and live a victorious life."

That's violent prayers. That's the kind of prayers we are going to pray in this book.

Chapter 2: Effects of Praying Violent Prayers

Bear in mind the three components of violent prayers. They are:

1. The Thought Process

2. The Push Factor

3. Authority.

There's got to be a decisive decision to change your life. There's got to be intensity in your thought that things must change. That you must get your healing, deliverance and breakthrough. You'll say to yourself, "enough is enough"

Once you have developed this thought process, then comes the PUSH factor. That is, being willing to pray until something happens...until you have some inner assurance that this matter is settled.

Jesus talked about this in a parable in Luke 18.

He said:

₂"In a certain town there was a judge who neither feared God nor cared what people thought. ₃And there was a widow in that town who kept coming to him with the plea, 'Grant me justice against my adversary.'

₄"For some time he refused. But finally he said to himself, 'Even though I don't fear God or care what people think, ₅yet because this widow keeps bothering me, I will see that she gets justice, so that she won't eventually come and attack me!'"

₆And the Lord said, "Listen to what the unjust judge says. ₇And will not God bring about justice for his chosen ones, who cry out to him day and night? Will he keep putting them off? ₈I tell you, he will see that they get justice, and quickly. However, when the Son of Man comes, will he find faith on the earth?"

The widow kept pressing until the stubborn king came down from his high position and enforced justice.

That's the push factor.

"That you prayed once and didn't see results doesn't mean you'll now resign to your situation. You'll have to PUSH for it. And you'll have to push for it with authority."

Let me share some examples of people who prayed violently and what the results were. From their stories, we can also see various types of violent prayers.

1. LORD, I'M DONE RUNNING.

Genesis 32:24-28:

So Jacob was left alone, and a man wrestled with him till daybreak.[25] When the man saw that he could not overpower him, he touched the socket of Jacob's hip so that his hip was wrenched as he wrestled with the man. ²⁶ Then the man said, "Let me go, for it is daybreak."

But Jacob replied, "I will not let you go unless you bless me."

²⁷ The man asked him, "What is your name?"

"Jacob," he answered.

²⁸ Then the man said, "Your name will no longer be Jacob, but Israel,[a] because you have struggled with God and with humans and have overcome."

That's what we are talking about. You won't let go just like that. You'll persist and overcome. You'll pray until you have an assurance in your spirit that this matter is taken care of.

Next.

We don't know exactly what was the problem with Jacob here that made him grab the angel and say, *"We've got to settle this matter once and for all. You either kill me or change me."*

The only thing we know is that before this time he was hiding, running away from his brother for fear of the repercussion of the fraud he meted out to him. That day he had gotten news that his brother was coming to meet him with four hundred soldiers.

Now, you don't go to see your blood brother with 400 fighting soldiers, all equipped, if all was well. Apparently sensing danger, Jacob had the option of running back to hide or face his fears. That night after he had put the women and children to sleep, he woke up and said,

"...LORD how long will I keep hiding? We've got to settle this matter, cos I'm going nowhere."

When the angel broke his waist, he must have said, *"Well, you should either kill me or change me. I need total deliverance from the consequences of the sin of my past. You're either giving me deliverance or give me death."*

That's violent prayers.

And Jacob won. When his brother finally saw him, his mind was already arrested in his favor.

Beloved, **anyone can get deliverance from any situation. It doesn't matter what sin you have committed in the past. Once you repent and give your life to Christ, you can be delivered**

from whatever is happening to you as a result of your past mistakes.

If the devil is still messing around, just get on with violent prayers.

2. LORD, TAKE THIS ANGUISH AWAY FROM ME.

You see, you are the only one who knows exactly where you are hurting. No matter how you try to explain it, sometimes you lack the exact words to let it out. Family, friends, and neighbors may be trying hard to comfort you, and that's great. But what is better is that the anguish, the pain, and the torment are taken away from you.

"It's better to get healed of your hurts and pains than to be consoled by friends and neighbors."

Take a look at Hannah. The husband did his best to console her. He stood by her at all times and encouraged her not to be bothered about her childlessness. As long as we are concerned, that's the best thing a woman needs when going through infertility. But no matter how great that kind of support is, it remains a temporary solution to the major problem.

One day, Hannah got fed up, left everyone to their merriment and hooked up with God at the temple. She didn't even bother to consult with the priest this time. As long as she was concerned, this matter has to be settled before God.

Now.

Not later.

She won't come back the same way next year. The Bible says:

> *¹²As she was praying to the LORD, Eli watched her. ¹³Seeing her lips moving but hearing no sound, he thought she had been drinking. – I Sam 1:12-13*

Can you see that! Even the priest who was expectedly filled with the Holy Spirit analyzed her wrongly.

That's what I keep saying. No one can pray for you like you will for yourself. Don't wait for someone to understand what you are saying entirely. Take your anguish to the LORD and refuse to give up until you experience a touch that will change your story. Until the peace and assurance of God fills your heart about whatever it is.

3. LORD, ENLARGE MY COAST.

There is a strange story in 1 Chronicles chapter 4: 1-9. Why I said strange is because one man there broke the sequence of records and stood out. From the verse one of that chapter, the writer was writing the history of a particular lineage. He was just saying things like, "this man **begath** this man, then this man had this number of children." And nothing else. He was just telling us the history of how some clans came to be in Judah.

But in verse 9, there was a deviation of the storyline. It says:

> *9Jabez was more honorable than his brothers. His mother had named him Jabez,[c] saying, "I gave birth to him in pain." 10Jabez cried out to the God of Israel, "Oh, that you would bless me and enlarge my territory! Let your*

*hand be with me, and keep me from harm so that I will be free from pain." And God granted his request. - **1 Chronicles 4: 9.***

Jabez had troubles and pains right from birth. In fact, the reason his mother named him Jabez was because he was born in pain. So pains followed the guy all his life.

From his prayers, I believe the biggest pain he suffered was that of poverty and lack. But he engaged God violently, and his story changed. He became more honorable than those who were not born in pains. He became more noble than those born with silver spoon.

From this story you can see a couple of things:

First, it's right to ask God to bless you financially. Praying for a breakthrough is okay. It's scriptural to ask God for business ideas and to enlarge your territory; that is, to expand your business into other nations.

God delights in the prosperity of his people (Psalm 35:27). He is happy when we are successful in business and are making money, taking care of our families and supporting His work. In fact, the scripture says that God is committed to blessing the works our hands.

So if it seems like you are struggling with your job or business, you can engage in violent prayers and let God guide you on the next things to do. If it seems you are struggling financially, you can go to God like Jabez and say, *"LORD, this is not right. I'm struggling. Help me. Show me what to do. Lead me to expand my business and career."*

The thing is that if you don't pray, and persist, nothing will happen. If you accept your situation and relax because you are just getting by with peanuts or social support, you'll remain just like that. And that is not God's will for your life.

Secondly, even if your financial problem is from your lineage, the curse can be broken, and you will begin to succeed.

Jabez' pain started from his birth. In fact, the Hebrew meaning of the name, Jabez, is **sorrow, trouble**. Why a parent will give a child that kind of name is still baffling to me. Even if she had him in great sorrow, naming the child sorrow was not right.

That was like a mother telling her child, *"I bore you in sorrow, so sorrow and trouble will follow you."* That's not right. In my culture, she would have named the child, "consolation of my sorrow," thus, invoking the power of comfort over the child.

But whatever the case is, there is still deliverance available if you call unto God in faith and persist. Even if your condition is a generational mark and stigma, it can be broken. You can obtain deliverance with violent prayers.

4. LORD, HEAL ME OF THIS DISEASE

Another case of violent prayer in practice is found Mark 5:25-34. There are variations of the same story in other Gospels but they share the same end. In the story, we find a woman who was suffering from what the Bible terms "issue of blood." That's more like "hemorrhage" in modern language, meaning, "continual outflowing of blood from a person."

I can imagine how this woman would be emotionally devastated from the social stigma that the sickness brought her. A person that blood is flowing out from every moment would not stay with people, not just for her pain, but for the shame of always having to see blood coming out of her.

In fact, the Jewish culture regarded such persons as unclean and forbade them from coming out to mingle with people. That means that culture was against her.

On the treatment side, the Bible says:

> *She had suffered a great deal under the care of many doctors and had spent all she had, yet instead of getting better she grew worse. – Mark 5:26*

This woman did everything to get cure from hospitals, but instead, she got worse. Then she heard about JESUS and decided to break free from the cultural cage and seek help from the master. She would not allow the multitude who thronged around Jesus to discourage her. Neither would she let the Jewish law which forbade her from mingling with people to stop her.

As long as she was concerned, she was done with shame. She must get to the master, if not officially, then unofficially. She pressed until she could lay hold of the master's garment. And the Bible says she was made whole instantly.

That's violent prayers.

You just have to leave your comfort zone and seek help from Christ who can help you. You have to press and never allow the crowd and culture to stop you from seeking Christ for help. As you do, you'll trigger chains of events that will bring you healing from whatever it is you are suffering from.

We bless God for doctors. They are doing great jobs. We need to appreciate them. Without doctors, we would have had more deaths from common ailments in this world.

But then, we also have to recognize their limitations. While getting treated, we should also acknowledge the place of prayer of faith. I believe that while doctors do their jobs, and we pray, the devil loses his grips and we regain our total health.

The Message

Violent prayers can set you free from your fears and consequences of your past mistakes, like Jacob.

Violent prayers can take away your unexplainable anguish, like Hannah.

Violent prayers can give you breakthrough, like Jabez.

And violent prayers can bring you healing of your body, like the hemorrhaging woman.

It's time to pray violently.

Chapter 3: **When You Need to Pray Violent Prayers and Minister Deliverance to Yourself or Home**

Now you know what violent prayers are. Now you know what violent prayers can achieve. So when do you need to pray violent prayers?

1. When you need healing.
2. When you need business and financial breakthrough.
3. When you need God to take anguish away from you.
4. When you need deliverance from demonic oppression.
5. When you sense that your home or where you live is under attack
6. When you detect generational strongholds

Let's look at these situations briefly.

1. WHEN YOU NEED HEALING.

If you need healing, then you need to pray violent prayers. As stated above, while we give ourselves to doctors to administer treatment, we also recognize their limitations. So we pray and stand on God's Words and claim our healing and health.

There are also other situations where the doctors can't seem to figure out what's wrong. At such times we must know those are a strong indication of demonic affliction that needs to be destroyed in Jesus name. The Bible says:

> *"And ought not this woman, being a daughter of Abraham, whom Satan hath bound, lo, these eighteen years, be loosed from this bond on the sabbath day? – Luke 13:16 (KJV)*

The woman in question here was afflicted by the spirit of infirmity, which made her bowed for 18 long years. After Jesus cast the spirit out and laid hands on her and prayed, she was healed.

Some sicknesses and diseases can be a result of evil spirit affliction. Such illnesses and pains usually defy medical analysis. When we face such cases, what we need is to embark on violent prayers and resist the devil

2. WHEN YOU NEED BUSINESS AND FINANCIAL BREAKTHROUGH.

Jabez needed a financial breakthrough. He prayed, and God answered his prayers and made him an honorable man.

The same can be applied for any child of God. If where you are at the moment is not conducive enough for you financially, if you need an upgrade in your income, you can pray and persist in prayers and God will show you the way forward.

It is God's will to bless the works of your hand. In fact, God wants us to expand beyond our country. Ecclesiastes 11:1-2 says:

> *Ship your grain across the sea; after many days you may receive a return. Invest in seven ventures, yes, in eight; you do not know what disaster may come upon the land. (NIV)*

This scripture simply means that it's possible for recession and other kinds of disasters to come on the land, but that if you invest in seven ventures, even eight, you'll be spared. That's more like saying, "invest in multiple streams of income. That's the only way to beat recession."

I believe this scripture, same way I believe John 3:16. I believe and teach that Christians need to have investment and business mindset. I believe that if you have one business today, God wants you to expand and have other businesses.

If your job is breaking your head and not leading you where you want, if your business is beating you up and down, you may need to engage in violent prayers and ask God for fresh ideas and breakthrough. It's God's delight to prosper you (Job 36:11, Psalm 35:27).

3. WHEN YOU NEED GOD TO TAKE ANGUISH AWAY FROM YOU.

The dictionary defines anguish as severe mental or physical pain or suffering. Other words related to anguish are agony, pain, torment, torture, suffering, distress, angst, misery, sorrow, grief, heartache, desolation, despair.

Anguish is a situation of pain and sorrowful condition that only you know exactly what's happening to you. The doctor or specialist may be offering treatment and encouragement, but you know deep down that you need more than that. Your loved ones may be encouraging you, but they don't fully understand what you are going through. Such anguish may be caused by an oppression, an expectation that is unnecessarily delayed, the loss of someone or something dear to you, or a need in your life that is not met.

Sometimes, you may not even know precisely how to express your pain. But you know you need healing and comfort. Whatever the case is, in moments that you seem so deep in sadness and pain, you can go to God in prayers and find comfort and healing. Hannah prayed from her heart and wept before that LORD. She said:

> *Don't think I am a wicked woman! For I have been praying out of great anguish and sorrow." – 1 Samuel 1:16.*

Take your anguish to the LORD and be rest assured that He will deliver you and you will praise Him. David said, "I sought the LORD, and he heard me, and delivered me from all my fears." (Psalm 34:4)

4. WHEN YOU NEED DELIVERANCE FROM DEMONIC OPPRESSIONS.

You need violent prayers to be free from demonic oppression.

But the first question is "how do I know if what I'm going through is a case of demonic oppression?"

Demonic oppressions can manifest in different forms, but three key elements help us to identify them. They are:

a. Fruits that are not of the Holy Spirit and God's promises

b. Discernment

c. The demonic oppression test

Let's try and explain what these things mean.

A. FRUITS THAT ARE NOT OF THE HOLY SPIRIT AND GOD'S PROMISES.

For instance, the fruits of the Holy Spirit include love, peace, joy, hope, faithfulness, patience and self-control (Galatians 5:22-23). If you suddenly see your life producing fruits contrary to these fruits, then you may be under demonic oppression. Take a look at the table below:

FRUITS OF THE SPIRIT	OPPOSITE
Love	animosity, dislike, enmity, hate, hatred, ill will, indifference, neglect, apathy, coolness, disloyalty, misery, sorrow, treachery, unhappiness
Joy	depression, misery, sadness, sorrow, unhappiness, discouragement, dislike, mourning,
Peace	disagreement, discord, agitation, disharmony, distress, fighting, frustration, upset, war, worry
Forbearance	agitation, excess, impatience, indulgence, intemperance, intolerance, wildness, involvement,
Kindness	hostility, indecency, indifference, intolerance, meanness, mercilessness, selfishness, thoughtlessness, barbarousness, cruelty, harshness

Goodness	corruption, cruelty, dishonesty, dishonor, evil, immorality, meanness, handicap, hindrance, loss, indecency, wickedness
Faithfulness	disloyalty, treachery, disregard, inconstancy, dishonesty, falseness
Gentleness	hardness, imperviousness, roughness
Self-control	gratification, indulgence, self-indulgence; excessiveness, immoderacy, intemperance, intemperateness, overindulgence; unrestraint

This table gives you an idea of when the fruits of evil spirits are cropping up in your life and you need to resist them violently.

I've classified the result from that table into internal and external signs that show you need deliverance or violent prayers. The internal signs are developments within you, while the external signs are developments outside of you.

a1.) INTERNAL DEVELOPMENTS THAT POINT TO A NEED FOR DELIVERANCE AND VIOLENT PRAYERS.

- If you suddenly see yourself developing hatred for the things of God or an unforgiveness in your heart over an offense against you that refuses to leave, that is anti-love spirit in operation, you may need to pray violent prayers to command back your freedom.

- If you suddenly start getting depressed, feeling hopeless, discouraged and separated, that is anti-joy spirit working; you need violent prayers and deliverance.

- If you suddenly start having severe disagreements in your home, become worrisome, develop the urge to fight back at any offence, that is anti-peace spirit in operation, you need deliverance.

- If you suddenly start losing your cool and patience with people and start getting agitated over trivial issues; if you suddenly start talking excessively and become intemperate, intolerant, wild and start tilting towards things you stopped doing in the past, that is anti-forbearance spirit in operation, you need deliverance.

- If you suddenly start admiring and loving immorality, porn, indecency, that is anti-goodness spirit working; you need deliverance.

- If corruption, dishonesty, and falseness suddenly start to appeal to you, that is anti-faithfulness spirit working; you need to break that yoke violently.

- If you just suddenly became mean and no longer feel remorse when you do wrong things, no longer show affection, empathy, and care over the hurt of others, that is the work of ant-kindness and gentleness spirit; you need to pray violently and claim your deliverance.

- If you are addicted to food, alcohol, dressing, TV, etc. ...Note that by addiction we mean doing things in excess, a point where it seems you can't live without those things, then you need deliverance.

a2.) EXTERNAL DEVELOPMENTS THAT POINT TO A NEED FOR DELIVERANCE AND VIOLENT PRAYERS.

The devil is the father of hate, war, fights, disagreements, disloyalty, corruption, worry, sorrow, depression, etc.

Sometimes he may work these things out to oppose you from others, not from within you.

For example, the devil can create events where people just hate you for nothing. Whatever you do, no one sees it as good. Your good works don't seem to be noticed, no matter how you try. Instead of you getting a raise, you get queries.

He may work out severe hostility, strife, and opposition towards you and your works in the workplace.

He may raise the spirit of falsehood and lies against you everywhere.

These external developments where the devil infiltrates people with wrong spirits that fights to stop you need violent prayers to address.

Remember:

> *"For we wrestle not against flesh and blood, but against principalities, against powers, against the rulers of the darkness of this world, against spiritual wickedness in high places."* - Ephesians 6:12

B. DISCERNMENT

We can also determine if a situation is a case of demonic oppression by discernment, which is an ability to sense that something is right or wrong somehow.

Something may be happening to you, in you or in your family and somehow, something in you is persuaded that this is not right. This is not how things are supposed to be. You may just sense some cloud of darkness hovering. Your prayers seems to be hitting the walls and things keep getting messier. In such situations violent prayers can help.

Asking the Holy Spirit to show and direct you to what is happening helps a lot.

C. DEMONIC OPPRESSION TEST.

Pastor Nate Thompson of Deliverance Revolution listed out what he calls Demonic Oppression Test. He suggests that when you notice any of these signs in your life, you may need violent prayers for deliverance. They are:

- A compulsive desire to blaspheme God

- A revulsion against the Bible, including a desire to tear it up or destroy it

- Compulsive thoughts of suicide or murder

- Deep feeling of resentment and hatred toward others without reason – Jews, other races, the church, strong Christian leaders

- Any compulsive temptations that seek to force thoughts or behavior that the person truly does not want to think or do

- Uncontrollable desires to tear other people down, even if it means lying to do so; vicious cutting by the tongue

- Disturbing feelings of guilt even after true confession is made to the Lord

- Specific physical symptoms that may appear suddenly or leave quickly and for which there are no physical or physiological reason

- Symptoms such as choking sensations, pains that seem to move around and for which there is no medical cause

- Sensation of tightness about the head or eyes, dizziness, blackouts, or fainting of hostility

- Deep depression and hopelessness

- Sudden surges of violent rage, uncontrollable anger, or seething feeling of hatred

- Sudden panic type feeling over your salvation, even though you remember being saved and saying the salvation prayer

- Seizures, panic or other fear type seizures that would be classified as terrifying

- Dreams or nightmares that are of a horrific in nature and often recurring

- Abnormal or perverted sexual desires

- Questions and challenges to God's Word

- Sleep or eating disorders without physical cause

- Bizarre, terrifying thoughts that seem to come from nowhere and cannot be controlled

- Fascination with the occult

- Involvement in criminal activity

- Extremely low self-esteem

- Constant confusion in thinking

- Inability to believe (even when you want to believe)

- Mocking and blasphemous thoughts against preaching/teaching of God

- Perception is distorted-perceiving anger or hostility in others

- Violent thoughts (suicidal, homicidal, self-abuse)

- Hatred and bitterness toward others for no justifiable reason

- Tremendous hostility or fear when encountering someone involved in Deliverance work

- Irrational fears, panic attacks, and phobias

- Irrational anger or rage

- Irrational guilt or self-condemnation to the extreme

- Yearning to do what is right but an inability to carry it out

- A strong aversion toward Scripture reading and prayer

- Sudden personality and attitude change – severe contrast, schizophrenia, bipolar disorder

- A dark countenance – steely or hollow look in eyes, contraction of the pupils sometimes facial features contort or change: often an inability to make eye contact

- Lying, exaggerating, or stealing on impulse, and often wondering why

- Eating obsessions – bulimia, anorexia nervosa

- Irrational violence, compulsion to hurt self and/or someone else

- Sudden speaking of a language not previously known (often an ethnic language of ancestors)

- Negative reaction to the name and blood of Jesus Christ (verbally or through body language)

- Extreme restlessness, especially in a spiritual environment

- Uncontrollable cutting and mocking tongue

- Vulgar language and actions

- Extreme sleepiness around spiritual things

- Demonstrating extraordinary abilities (either ESP or telekinesis)

- Voices heard in the mind that mock, intimidate, accuse, threaten or attempt to bargain

- Supernatural experiences – hauntings, movements or disappearance of object and other strange manifestations

- Seizures (too long and/or too regular)

- Pain without reasonable explanation, especially in head or stomach

- Memory Blackouts

- Physical ailments such as epileptic seizures, asthma attacks, and various strains

- Sudden temporary interference with bodily function – buzzing in ears, inability to speak or hear, severe headache, hypersensitivity in hearing or touch chills or overwhelming heat in body, numbness in arms or legs, temporary paralysis

If you can relate with any of the issues raised so far, buckle up and let's get on with some violent prayers and enforce your freedom in Jesus Christ.

5. WHEN YOU DETECT THAT YOUR HOME, OR OFFICE, OR PROPERTY, OR WHERE YOU LIVE IS UNDER DEMONIC ATTACK.

Demons can invade a home, building, an environment or property and cause some problems for the occupants of that property. They are usually able to do that when there has been some doorways for them.

"Demonic doorways are simply things that give evil spirits access into a person's house, property or life. These things could be covenants, consulting witch doctors, unholy agreements, using items dedicated to demons, etc.

"It is important to note that **not knowing that something is existing does not stop it from existing.** That one does not know that something was used for demonic purposes and brings it into his house does not prevent the fact that the thing was used for satanic purposes. But the good news is that when we pray, the power of God will neutralize whatever is not of God and deliver victory into our hands.

The Bible says:

The graven images of their gods you shall burn with fire. You shall not desire the silver or gold that is on them, nor take it for yourselves, lest you be ensnared by it, for it is an abomination to the Lord your God.

Neither shall you bring an abomination (an idol) into your house, lest you become an accursed thing like it; but you shall utterly detest and abhor it, for it is an accursed thing. - **Deuteronomy 7:25-26 (AMP)**

"God is simply telling His people here that they could come under a curse and suffer if they bring into their houses things used for idol worship. Things like books, drawings, replicas, etc.

This also means that if a person relocates to a house that was used for idol worship, he could come **"under the ban"** if he does not remove these accursed things. It is the process of removing these accursed things that is called family deliverance or home cleansing prayers.

"Some people have asked and said, *"How can I detect the exact things that are the doorways for evil spirits into my life and home?"*

"The truth is that it may require the leading of the Holy Spirit to be able to tell the exact access point of evil spirits into a place or person's life, especially where the person or persons involved are Christians and serving the LORD. When we pray with open mind and seek the

LORD, the Holy Spirit will lead us to make the right call and take away what belongs to the devil that is in our possession.

"It is also important to know that even when we couldn't find any objects to remove, we must believe our prayers and not entertain fear. We must stand in our victory and keep praising God for our freedom in Christ.

"All through the Bible, we see the practice of dedicating persons, buildings, properties and belongings to God as a frequent necessity. When something is dedicated to God, it becomes holy unto the LORD. When Jesus was born, He was dedicated to God. (Luke 2:22-40).

"Witches, wizards, witch doctors, necromancers, stargazers, occult men, and women dedicate their lives and properties to the devil. When people go to live in such places already dedicated to the devil, they may come under spiritual attacks and oppression.

"When we pray for cleansing of a home or property, what we are saying, in essence, is,

" You satan, demons, and evil spirits, get off his home, get off this property, in Jesus name! Henceforth, this house belongs to the LORD. This car, this office, this

property, everything here belongs to the LORD. Whatever you are holding as leverage is hereby destroyed. Now leave, in Jesus name."

6. WHEN YOU PERCEIVE GENERATIONAL STRONGHOLDS.

You also need to pray violent prayers when you notice a generational problem in your life or family.

Generational strongholds or bondages or problems are issues passed from one generation of a family to another generation. Just like a family can bequeath wealth and business to the next generation, specific weaknesses and negativities in a family can be passed on from past generations to other generations.

That's why sometimes, doctors, in treating certain sicknesses will look at your family history. If a family has a history of cancer or diabetes or any other thing, the doctors want to know how best to address the matter from the root.

Have you ever seen a family where the father is having a problem with uncontrollable anger, his son seems to have it as well, and the granddad had the same problem?

Or have you detected that not only do you suffer from something such as insistent, irrational fears or depression, but your mother and her father also had the same problem?

Those are effects produced by ancestral connections. They are beyond learned behaviors; they are bondages that must be intentionally broken with violent prayers.

Another example of common symptoms of ancestral curses are family illnesses that seem to just walk from one person down to the next, continual financial difficulties, mental problems, persistent, irrational fears, and depression, etc.

So if you suspect that a situation happening in your home has some connection with your lineage, you need violent prayers to detach your family from that connection.

Chapter 4: How to Minister Deliverance to Yourself or to Someone Else

Binding and casting out demons is not an unusual thing. **Any Christian, who can pray "THE LORD'S PRAYER" can cast out the devil and obtain deliverance for anyone when they pray.** There is no need making it look like it's a big deal.

Jesus said:

> *"...I saw Satan fall like lightning from heaven. See, I have given you authority to tread on snakes and scorpions, and over all the power of the enemy. Nothing will harm you.*
>
> *"Nevertheless, do not rejoice that the spirits submit to you, but rejoice that your names are written in heaven."... (Luke 10:18-20)*

Those who receive Christ as their LORD and savior have their names written in the Book of Life. They can bind and cast out demons and nothing shall by any means hurt them.

You can violently bind and cast out the devil from your life and family as a child of God. Yes, you can and should learn to do that. In fact, the book of Proverbs said:

> *Deliver thyself as a roe from the hand of the hunter, and as a bird from the hand of the fowler.* **Proverbs 6:5**

You can and should deliver yourself. No one can pray for you the way you will for yourself. You hold the key into your life. Whatever you forbid will be forbidden, and whatever you allow will be allowed. So here are the steps to minister deliverance to yourself or to a loved one.

1. IF POSSIBLE, GET SOMEONE TO AGREE WITH YOU.

Hold on. If you are ministering personal deliverance to yourself, you can actually pray alone. But if you are ministering to your home, office or property, you can get someone to join you. Usually, whether personal deliverance or family or property deliverance, two are usually better than one. Jesus said in Matthew 18:19 that ...

> *"If two of you shall agree on earth as touching anything that they shall ask, it shall be done for them of my Father which is in heaven."*

Again Ecclesiastes 4:9-12 has this to say:

> *Two are better than one, because they have a good return for their labor: If either of them falls down, one can help the other up. But pity anyone who falls and has no one to help them up.*
>
> *Also, if two lie down together, they will keep warm. But how can one keep warm alone? Though one may be overpowered, two can defend themselves. A cord of three strands is not quickly broken.*

There is power in a prayer of agreement.

But please note, while this is important, it is not compulsory. You are the one who needs freedom and you can demand it in Jesus name and get it.

2. FAST AND PRAY

You are embarking on a mission to dislodge the powers of darkness from your life and environment, so a good spiritual preparation is necessary to give way to the Holy Spirit. Jesus said that there are stubborn demons that will try to resist our prayers, but with fasting we can be adequately prepared to crush them. (Matthew 17:21). Fasting increases the power of prayer several times over.

When you fast, ask the Holy Spirit to open your eyes to doorways that needs to be removed. Humble yourself before God and receive direction to approach the prayer sessions.

3. LOCATE EVERY EVIL DOORWAY AND DEAL WITH IT.

Ask the Holy Spirit to show you what open doors you might have that would allow evil spirits to oppress you or come into your home. He will show you things and areas that need to be addressed.

Some common examples of demonic doorways are: porn, occult books, covenanted rings, objects used in witchcraft, willful disobedience to the leading of the Holy Spirit, addictions, secret sins, satanic movies and even objects.

Some doorways may be sins, while others may be unknown objects somewhere in the house or property. As you pray, and follow the leading of the Holy Spirit, He'll put it in your heart, areas that you may need to confess sins to the LORD or things to take away and destroy.

Just be open to the Holy Spirit to show you what needs to be done here. The Bible says:

> *"Many who had believed now came forward, confessing and disclosing their deeds. And a number of those who had practiced magic arts brought their books and burned them in front of everyone. When the value of the books was calculated, it came to fifty*

thousand drachmas. So the word of the Lord powerfully continued to spread and prevail"

- Acts 19:18-20

4. LEVERAGE ON 'THE POWER OF THE NIGHT'

The night hours are victory hours. What happens in the NIGHT TIMES usually determines the results of the day. That is why occult people mainly have their meetings in the night.

The Bible says in Psalm 91:5:

> *You will not fear the terror of night, nor the arrow that flies by day*

That simply means that terrors are usually executed in the night times. You know why? Because *"Everyone who does evil hates the day, and will not come into the light for fear that their deeds will be exposed* (John 3:30-Paraphrased).

Jesus said in Matthew 13:25...

> *But while men slept, his enemy came and sowed tares among the wheat, and went his way.*

Enemies utilize the night to sow tares in people's lives because they easily get away without notice. But when we decide to watch and pray in the night, we can destroy whatever the enemies have sown and release our hanging blessings.

5. ALL THE PRAYERS.

There are about several prayer points in the prayer chapters below arranged as a 3 days guide. They range from confession prayers, declaration prayers, and deliverance prayers to prayers of intercession for your family. I advise that you pray all the prayers for each prayer session.

Basically, in these 3 days of violent prayers, you will claim your deliverance, healing and breakthrough.

6. PRAY WITH THE WORD.

This book will help you pray with the word of God

effectively. Your prayers will have more power and produce more effect when they are saturated with God's Word.

So, in praying the prayers in this book take time to read the scriptures that are recommended and personalize them. If after reading a scripture, you feel like praying some other way before coming back to this outline, that's okay.

7. PRAY WITH AUTHORITY.

Please do not recite the prayer points in this book. That is, do not just read them only and say you have prayed. The prayer points are just guides. As you read out one, spend time praying it through with words the Holy Spirit puts in your mouth.

And if you are baptized in the Holy Spirit, do not hesitate to pray in tongues whenever you are moved, even while you follow the prayer points and strategies in this book (see Ephesians 6:18, jude20).

8. MAINTAIN A GOOD POSITION.

There is no specific position you must stay while praying. You can stay anyhow you want. You can pray sitting down, walking, lying down, etc. But when you are doing serious warfare, like that of personal or family deliverance and property cleansing, standing and walking around is usually better. However, don't feel bad if you sit down and pray

9. BE SENSITIVE AND PRAY WITH A NOTE.

During this season you separate to pray out yourself and your family from the wicked works of the devil, you will have some revelations, either in dreams, trance or a serious impression or insight while reading the bible. These may contain vital instructions you need to carry out. When you have such insights or revelations, write them down. And quickly set about doing them.

They may come in form of ideas, dream, or a thought on what to about the situation. However they come, recognize what God is saying and do them. That is what gets prayers answered quickly.

10. USE THE ANOINTING OIL

Get yourself a bottle of the ANOINTING oil. You are going to anoint yourself and your environment and dedicate it to God.

The Bible has a lot to say about anointing with oil. It's used to invoke healing, protection, dedication, favor and divine enablement (see the following scriptures:

- Samuel 10:1-7, 16:13,
- Mark 6:12-13,
- James 5:14-15)

PART 2:

3 Days Fasting and Prayers Guide for Deliverance, Healing and Breakthrough

Chapter 5: Instructions for Praying

1. Spend a few minutes in praise and worship to the Lord before praying

2. Confess any known sin to the Lord

3. Ask the Lord to bring to your memory the legal ground or the doors that the forces of spiritual wickedness are using to gain entrance into your life and family.

4. Where you have found the demonic doorways, remove them before praying.

5. If you have any issue with anyone, forgive and ask God for grace to be free from anger and bitterness towards the people who have offended you.

6. Believe in your prayers. Believe that your prayers will work.

Chapter 6: Day 1:

Prayers of Confession, Forgiveness, Rededication, Holy Spirit Empowerment, and Deliverance from Bad Habits and Addictions

Instruction:

Today is the first day of your violent prayers for deliverance, healing and breakthrough. It is important that you start today with confessing your sins to the LORD and rededicating your life to Him.

It is also important that today be a day you present any bad habit or addictions in your life that is a gateway for the devil to oppress you. When our ways are clean before the LORD we can place a demand on God's power for our deliverance and breakthrough. That is what we will achieve today.

Note: Always begin each of your prayer sessions with

praises and thanksgiving to God. This sets the atmosphere right for supernatural manifestation.

SCRIPTURES

Read Psalm 51: 1-19

PRAYERS: SESSION 1

1. *"Heavenly Father, have mercy upon my life. I believe and confess that Jesus is your only begotten son through whom we obtain salvation. Forgive me of all my sins and cleanse me with the precious blood of Jesus Christ, in Jesus name.*

---

2. *O Lord, create in me a new heart, a heart that will always seek after you. Let your Spirit take over my life and direct me from today forward. Lead me on the path of righteousness and cause me to live a holy and consecrated life to THEE. In Jesus name.*

---

3. *From today, O LORD JESUS, I am separated from sin. I confess that Jesus Christ is my Lord and my savior. I am now a new creature. Old things have passed away .I will grow daily in the knowledge of God from today, in the Mighty name of Jesus Christ*

READ:

- John 14:15-18,

- John 15:26,

- John 16:13-14,

- Romans: 8:11--27

PRAYERS: SESSION 2

4. Dear Holy Spirit, I welcome you into my life. I surrender my spirit, soul and body unto You this moment. Let your presence be revealed in my life, in the mighty name of Jesus Christ.

---

5. Holy Spirit, open my spiritual ears. Cause me to walk in the path ordained to establish my destiny. May I never miss your leading and direction for my life from today in Jesus Name.

---

6. Holy Spirit, empower me all through this prayer session and direct me properly in the Glorious name of Jesus Christ.

---

7. Holy Ghost Fire, saturate this environment right now in Jesus name.

---

8. Every spirit of distraction and weakness, I bind and

cast you into abyss in Jesus name.

---

9. I forbid distraction and weakness of the body this movement. I have strength and power to wait on the Lord this night and all other coming nights. In Jesus name.

---

10. My LORD and my God, I immerse my spirit, soul and body completely in the blood of Jesus Christ right now. In Jesus name.

---

11. According to the book of Exodus 12:13 'the blood shall be to me for a token upon my life and family, and when the angel of death shall see the blood, he shall pass over and the plague shall not rest upon me and my house hold.'

According to the book of Revelation 12:11, **I overcome the enemy by the Blood of Jesus Christ.**

Therefore, I call upon the everlasting Blood of Jesus Christ right now to erect a wall of protection over my life and family in the name of Jesus Christ.

12. *According to Zechariah 9:11,* ***"by the blood of thy covenant I have sent forth thy prisoners out of the pit where is no water"***

Because of this Word of the Lord, I decree today that I have my freedom, deliverance, and breakthrough. By the Blood of Jesus Christ and His covenant, I am coming out of every pit where I have hitherto been buried. Whatever has been holding me from moving forward in life and possessing my possessions, I decree them nullified in Jesus name.

Thank You Jesus, for my victory, In Jesus name.

PRAYERS: SESSION 3

READ SCRIPTURES:

Romans 12:1-2: "I beseech you therefore, brethren, by the mercies of God, that ye present your bodies a living sacrifice, holy, acceptable unto God, [which is] your reasonable service.

"And be not conformed to this world: but be ye transformed by the renewing of your mind, that ye may prove what [is] that good, and acceptable, and perfect, will of God."

Psalm 1:1-3: "Blessed is the one who does not walk in step with the wicked or stand in the way that sinners take or sit in the company of mockers,

"But whose delight is in the law of the Lord, and who meditates on his law day and night.

"That person is like a tree planted by streams of water, which yields its fruit in season and whose leaf does not wither— whatever they do prospers.

2 Corinthians 10: 4-5: *The weapons we fight with are not the weapons of the world. On the contrary, they have divine power to demolish strongholds.*

We demolish arguments and every pretension that sets itself up against the knowledge of God, and we take captive every thought to make it obedient to Christ.

PRAYERS

1. Almighty Father, I surrender my body to you. I hand over my thoughts to you. I dedicate my mind, imagination and attitude to you henceforth, in Jesus name.

---

2. O LORD, uproot out of my life every inner argument and unbelief contesting your Word in my life, in Jesus name.

---

3. I hereby arrest every negative thought in me, resisting the move of the Holy Spirit. I command these thoughts to wither by fire in right now, in Jesus name.

4. Every spiritual stronghold in my life working against the knowledge of God, I pull you down right now, in the name of Jesus Christ.

5. I command all the false gods contesting for worship in my life, die by fire right now, in Jesus name.

6. Every bad habit in my life, causing a barrier between the power of God, O LORD, let your fire destroy them right now, in Jesus name.

7. From today LORD JESUS, plant in me an everlasting hatred for lust anger, bitterness, alcoholism, smoking, drinking, and over eating, in the mighty name of Jesus Christ.

8. I claim my freedom from every destructive habit. In Jesus name.

9. You spirits of anger, lust, dishonesty, lying, spiritual laziness, pride, exaggeration, alcoholism, smoking, gossiping, and criticizing – by the blood of Jesus, I am forever free from all of you. I command you all to leave my life now and go into the abyss in Jesus name.

---

10. O LORD my Father, whatever evil effect in my life, resulting from my characters, past mistakes, or addiction to negative thought, word and habits, LORD JESUS set free.

---

11. O LORD, whatever curse and obstacle my wrong association and friendships have brought upon my life, let them be destroyed today in the name of Jesus Christ.

---

12. Father, from now onwards, surround me with the right people – surround me with people who will challenge me towards a Godly and excellent life. In Jesus name.

---

13. "From today, Almighty father I commit myself never to walk in the counsel of the ungodly, nor stand in the way of sinners, nor dine with mockers.

---

14. *" I commit myself to delight in the word of God and fellowship. I shall henceforth depend on God's word day and night, and its power shall work in me always to bear the right fruits.*

---

15. *"I am like a tree planted by the side of the river. My strength shall not fail. From season to season I shall bear fruit... in Jesus Mighty name.*

THANK YOU JESUS FOR ANSWERED PRAYER.

Chapter 7: Day 2:

Prayers to Destroy Curses from Family Lineage, and Enforce Your Personal Deliverance from Demonic Attacks and Oppressions

INSTRUCTION.

Today is the second day of your three days prayers for deliverance and breakthrough.

Yesterday, you rededicated your life to the LORD and claimed your deliverance from bad habits.

Today, you are going to disconnect yourself from ancestral curses and obtain personal deliverance from demonic oppressions and attacks.

So brace up.

SCRIPTURES.

Jeremiah 31:28-30: *Just as I watched over them to uproot and tear down, and to overthrow, destroy and bring disaster, so I will watch over them to build and to plant," declares the LORD.*

29 "In those days people will no longer say, 'The parents have eaten sour grapes, and the children's teeth are set on edge.'

30Instead, everyone will die for their own sin; whoever eats sour grapes--their own teeth will be set on edge.

2 Corinthians 5:17: *Therefore if any man be in Christ, he is a new creature: old things are passed away; behold, all things are become new.*

Galatians 3:13-14: *"Christ redeemed us from the curse of the law by becoming a curse for us, for it is written: "Cursed is everyone who is hung on a pole."[a]*

"He redeemed us in order that the blessing given to Abraham might come to the Gentiles through Christ Jesus, so that by faith we might receive the promise of the Spirit.

PRAYERS: SESSION 1

1. Because I am in Christ Jesus, old things have passed away, all things have become new. Therefore, every form of childhood manipulation still working against my life, family, marriage and destiny, be destroyed in Jesus name.

2. Blood of Jesus, Flow right through to my point of origin, foundation and body system and cleanse me from all childhood defilement and evil inheritance. In Jesus name.

3. I set myself free from every problem and difficulty operating in my life as a result of ignorant childhood initiation and evil practice by my parents, grandparents and guardians, in Jesus name.

4. Every demonic seed and plantation deposited into my life and my body from my childhood, be roasted by fire in the name of Jesus.

5. *"According to the word of God, if a man be in Christ, he is new creation, old things are passed away, and all things are become new. I therefore announce this day before heaven and earth,*

"I am a child of God. Jesus is in my life. I have been removed from satanic kingdom and translated into the kingdom of light. I am a new creation, destined to succeed in everything I do. I cannot be stopped by anything. In Jesus name.

---

6. *"Every curse holding onto the covenant of my ancestors to chase my life and destiny, you are helpless. By the blood of Jesus Christ, I announce my total freedom from every one of you today, in Jesus name.*

---

7. *I command all familiar spirits perpetrating evils in my life and family, hindering the glory of God from showing forth in our efforts, be crippled this day and get into abyss in the name of Jesus Christ.*

8. Every demonic shrine, altar and temple existing in my life and family, be destroyed in the mighty name of Jesus.

---

9. O LORD my God, let every satanic covering and cloud of darkness over my life and family be completely destroyed right now, in Jesus name.

---

10. Every eater of flesh and drinker of bloood chasing my life and family, die by fire right now, in Jesus name.

---

11. *(Lay your hand on your stomach and pray):* I break every evil chord connecting me to the curses on the ancestors of my family and village, in the name of Jesus Christ.

---

12. From today, O LORD, according to Mathew 18:18, I forbid untimely death, sickness, barrenness, disappointment and failure in my life and family, in the mighty name of Jesus Christ.

13.

Let every closed door, opportunities and gift in my life and family open from today in the name Jesus Christ.

PRAYERS: SESSION2:

SCRIPTURES:

- 2Corinthians 6:14-17
- Colossians 1:13-14

PRAYERS

14. "O LORD, as it is written in Colossians 1:13-14, I have been translated from the kingdom of darkness into the kingdom of the son, Jesus Christ. In him I have redemption, through his blood, even the forgiveness of sins. I therefore make even the proclamation today before heaven and earth.

"I belong to a new kingdom, the kingdom of light. I am seated with Christ in the heavenly places, far above all principalities and powers. Nothing can stop me from manifesting the glory of God; nothing will stop me from being healed and walk in divine health. Thank You Lord Jesus. In Jesus name.

15. Every hidden covenant working against my life, family and destiny be destroyed in Jesus name.

---

16. Heavenly Father, I decree right now, whatever demonic instrument of accusation in my possession, knowingly or unknowingly, let their power be paralyzed today in Jesus name.

---

17. I call upon the fire of God right now to destroy permanently every hidden and unknown curse, spell, charm, incantations and evil statements made against my life and family in Jesus name.

---

18. I now belong to a new covenant of life, peace, health and prosperity sealed with the holy and powerful blood of Jesus Christ. In Jesus name.

PRAYERS: SESSION 3

SCRIPTURES

Psalm 125: 1-3: Those who trust in the Lord are like Mount Zion, which cannot be shaken but endures forever.

As the mountains surround Jerusalem, so the Lord surrounds his people both now and forevermore.

PRAYERS:

1. I banish all evil messengers and monitoring spirits from hell assigned against my life and family in Jesus name.

---

2. Every demonic messenger and monitoring spirit from hell assigned against my life and family, I paralyze all your powers and cast all of you into abyss in the Glorious name of Jesus Christ.

3. My father and my God, let a furious east wind from heaven scatter, confuse and paralyze every evil gathering against my life and my family, in Jesus name .

4. Every stubborn evil perpetrator in my life and family, die by fire in the name of Jesus Christ.

5. It is written in Isaiah 54:15-16 that **'they shall gather together, but not by God's ordination. Every gathering against me shall not stand.'**

I therefore decree, O LORD, let ever demonic court existing against my life and family be destroyed today by fire, in the name of Jesus Christ.

6. Every demonic lawyer and judge raising accusation against my life, family and destiny, wherever you are, I command you all to die in fire in the name of Jesus Christ.

7. I nullify every evil judgment and decision which has been raised against my life and destiny in Jesus name.

READ

Psalm 2:1-5: *Why do the heathen rage and the people imagine a vain thing?*

The kings of the earth set themselves, and the rulers take counsel together, against the Lord, and against his anointed, saying, Let us break their bands asunder, and cast away their cords from us.

He that sitteth in the heavens shall laugh: the Lord shall have them in derision.

Then shall he speak unto them in his wrath, and vex them in his sore displeasure.

....

Psalm 35: 1-8: *Plead my cause, O Lord, with them that strive with me: fight against them that fight against me. Take hold of shield and buckler, and stand up for mine help.*

Draw out also the spear, and stop the way against

them that persecute me: say unto my soul, I am thy salvation.

Let them be confounded and put to shame that seek after my soul: let them be turned back and brought to confusion that devise my hurt.

Let them be as chaff before the wind: and let the angel of the Lord chase them. Let their way be dark and slippery: and let the angel of the Lord persecute them.

For without cause have they hid for me their net in a pit, which without cause they have digged for my soul. Let destruction come upon him at unawares; and let his net that he hath hid catch himself: into that very destruction let him fall.

CONTINUE PRAYING

8. O lord, I will live to eat the fruit of my labor. Any man or woman, witch or wizard, who has vowed that I will not see good in life, let fire from heaven visit them and destroy their curses in Jesus name.

9. I command all spiritual arrows designed or released against me, my life and family and my marriage to go back to the sender in Jesus name.

---

10. Holy Ghost fire, visit and expose any evil man or woman working against my life and family this year in Jesus name.

---

11. Every grave dug against me and my family, O LORD, I close them in the mighty name of Jesus Christ.

---

12. May every curse, spell, charm, invoked against my life, may all the plans of the wicked agents of darkness; perish by fire today, in Jesus name.

---

13. Whatever belong to my life spiritually, physically and financially, that has be damaged by the curse and work of the wicked individuals be restored back sevenfold, in Jesus name.

Thank You Jesus.

Chapter 8: Day 3:

Prayers Against Self Imposed Curses, Challenges, Spiritual Attacks. and Ministering to Yourself

Today is the third day of your prayers.

Today is the day to revoke any curse you have placed on yourself unknowingly.

Today, you will challenge and send spiritual attacks packing and minister healing and deliverance to yourself with the anointing oil.

PRAYERS: SESSION 1

SCRPTURES:

Proverbs 18:21: *'The tongue can bring death or life; those who love to talk will reap the consequences.'*

Proverbs 13:2: *'From the fruit of a man's mouth he enjoys good, But the desire of the treacherous is violence.'*

Matthew 12:37: *"For by your words you will be acquitted, and by your words you will be condemned."*

PRAYERS

1. *O LORD, let the Blood of Jesus set me free from the clutch of negative statements and curses from my parents in the name of Jesus Christ.*

2. *LORD Jesus, set me free from every curse working*

against my life and destiny and limiting your goodness in my life from my parents, grandparents, teachers or those I have served in the past, in Jesus name.

---

3. Every curse I have brought upon myself through negative statements and confessions, O LORD forgive me and set me free today in Jesus name.

---

4. From today Holy Spirit, take over my life and help me to say the right things about God, myself, my family and others, in Jesus name.

---

5. Every demonic spirit projected from the pit of hell to manipulate and influence my dreams, I blind and cast you all into abyss in Jesus name.

---

6. All satanic voices of confusion and manipulation influencing my life in any way, I command you to cease from now onwards, in the mighty name of Jesus Christ.

7. O LORD, let your angels and visions be what surrounds my dreams from now onward in Jesus name.

8. Every spirit of anxiety, depression and oppression against my life and family members, I command you all to get out right now out of my life and family and descend into abyss, in Jesus name.

9. From today, I decree, according to Philippians 4:7, that **"the peace of God, which passes all understanding, will guard my hearts and my minds in Christ Jesus"**. *In Jesus name.*

10. LORD JESUS, you said in Matthew 11:28 that You will give everyone who is under labor rest. LORD, I receive your rest today. In Jesus name.

PRAYERS: SESSION 2:

In this session, you need to minister healing, deliverance and freedom to yourself and release Favor into your life and family.

SCRIPTURES:

Mathew 15:13: *But he answered and said, "Every plant, which my heavenly Father hath not planted, shall be rooted up."*

Exodus 23:25-26: *Worship the Lord your God, and his blessing will be on your food and water. I will take away sickness from among you, and none will miscarry or be barren in your land. I will give you a full life span.*

James 5:13-15: *Is any one of you suffering? He should pray. Is anyone cheerful? He should sing praises.*

Is any one of you sick? He should call the elders of the church to pray over him and anoint him with oil in the name of the Lord.

And the prayer offered in faith will restore the one who is sick. The Lord will raise him up. If he has sinned, he will be forgiven....

PRAYERS:

(Lay your hand upon your head)

1. *"O LORD, according to your word, every tree you have not planted shall be rooted out and every chaff burned with fire.*

   I therefor ask that the Fire of the Holy Spirit, trace every satanic seed and plantation in in my life and let them be destroyed, in Jesus name.

---

2. *"Every seed of laziness, disappointment, spiritual deafness, bareness, sin, confusion, frustration and setback, be destroyed today by fire in the name of Jesus Christ.*

3. LORD, it is written that as I serve You, You will take sickness and disease away from me and my family and none shall be barren.

It is also written in 3 John 1: 2 that You want us to prosper and be in good health. And in Psalm 107: 20, that You sent Your Word, and Your Word heals us from every disease.

I therefore pray this moment LORD, take away every sickness and diseases from me. Take away this sickness from………. (CALL NAMES). In Jesus name.

---

4. O LORD, I ask that your Spirit will energize me from today and help me to always listen to your voice and harken to your instruction and commands. Help me to always study Your Word and follow your direction for my life. And by this I confess that I will live the days of my life in health in Jesus name.

---

5. It is written in Isaiah 53:4-5 and 2 peter 2:24 that **"Christ took away my sorrows and carried my infirmities and diseases in his body at the**

cross. He was pierced for my sins and inabilities. The punishment and blow he suffered on the cross was for the peace. By his strips I am healed."

I therefore anoint myself according to the WORD of God; O LORD, let your healing power move all over my body right now in Jesus name.

---

6. Every spirit behind this disease and affliction, I curse you in the name of the lord, and I command you to leave my life right now in Jesus name.

---

7. I command this sickness (name it) to wither out of my body this moment in Jesus mighty name.

---

8. It is written in Job 22:28, that I shall decree a thing and it shall be established, and light will shine on my ways. It is also written in the Mathew 18:18 that whatever I forbid here on earth will be forbidden in heaven and what I approve of will approved.

I therefore decree an end to all forms of spiritual

attacks in my life and family today. In Jesus name.

---

9. You evil spirit fighting and oppressing my life, family, business, finance, dreams and spiritual life, I bind and cast you all into abyss in Jesus name.

---

10. It is written that whoever the son sets free shall be free indeed. Jesus has set me free, I am free indeed. My family is free, my body is free, my children are free, my business and my marriage and my career are set free. My destiny is set free to shine from now onwards ....in the name of Jesus Christ.

PRAYERS: SESSION 3:

SCRIPTURES

- Exodus 23:25-26,
- Deut.7:14-15,
- Psalm 57:2-3,
- Psalm 113
- Psalm 127:3

SING AND WORSHIP.

Worship and thank God for His Word which must be fulfilled in your life.

PRAYERS:

11. *O LORD, according to Your Words, bareness and infertility is not my inheritance.*

As I take this short of anointing oil, Let the power of God flow into every part of my organ and system right now, and let every yoke of bareness, fibroid, miscarriage, infertility and unfruitfulness be destroyed, in Jesus name.

---

12. Every evil spirit organized and projected to enforce bareness, miscarriage, shame and delay in my life and family, I bind and cast you all into abyss in Jesus name.

---

13. O my Father, this month is my month of breakthrough. According to Genesis 1:28, I have a covenant with fruitfulness.

Therefore LORD, let my bowel open. My child must come this moment. (Tell God what you want and thank him for granting your request.). In Jesus name.

PRAYERS: SESSION 4

Releasing the anointing of favor and breakthrough into your life.

SCRIPTURES:

- Psalm 5:12,
- Psalm 30:5,
- Psalm 89:17,
- Psalm 102:12,
- Ephesians 3:2,
- Matthew 7:7-11

14. *O LORD, I thank You for your Words. According to what I have read here in Your Words right now, favor is your plan for my life. And the time for my favor and breakthrough is now.*

So I decree LORD, from today, wherever I go my voice shall be heard. I shall no longer labor in darkness. The light of heaven will shine on my ways. My presence shall be desired in important places from now onwards. In Jesus name.

---

15. I shall walk in wisdom, knowledge and the fear of God. I shall not die before my time. I shall live and continue to declare the goodness of the lord. In Jesus name.

---

16. The wind of favor is blowing in every aspect of my life and family; I shall walk in financial prosperity from now onwards. Everyone and everything is working for my good, In Jesus name.

Deliverance from every demonic Oppression

· healing in my body

· salvation, Baptism of Holy Ghost / Fire deliverance for John/Keira, Christian

PRESENT YOUR WRITTEN REQUESTS TO THE LORD:

Pick up that sheet of paper where you wrote some specific things you desire from God before entering into this prayer covenant.

Read the following three passages again. With the promises of these passages pray over those things one by one.

- Mathew 7:7-11.
- Ephesian3:20,

Now to him who is able to do immeasurably more than we all ask or imagine according to his power that is at work within us.

- Luke 1:37.

For no word from God will ever fail

Finally, spend some time and worship and thank the LORD for answering your prayers.

· repentance and salvation and deliverance for my dad / Noelle

· deliverance, Baptism of Holy Spirit for Mom / Ronnie

Chapter 9: Bring to God an Offering of Midnight Praise

You've just gone through a 3 days violent prayer session. Today is the 4th day. So it's a day of praise. Dedicate today and give God an offering of high praises. Praise God and dance before HIM for your victory and deliverance.

SCRIPTURES

Isaiah 25:1: *Lord, you are my God; I will exalt you and praise your name, for in perfect faithfulness you have done wonderful things, things planned long ago.*

Acts 16: 25-26: *About midnight Paul and Silas were praying and singing hymns to God, and the other prisoners were listening to them.*

Suddenly there was such a violent earthquake that the

foundations of the prison were shaken. At once all the prison doors flew open, and everyone's chains came loose.

✴ **Psalm 103:1-5:** *Praise the Lord, my soul; all my inmost being, praise his holy name.*

Praise the Lord, my soul, and forget not all his benefits—

Who forgives all your sins and heals all your diseases,

Who redeems your life from the pit and crowns you with love and compassion,

Who satisfies your desires with good things so that your youth is renewed like the eagle's.

PRAYERS

1. It is written in Obadiah 1:17**: But upon mount Zion shall be deliverance, and there shall be**

holiness; and the house of Jacob shall possess their possessions.

Thank You Jehovah for my deliverance. I am now possessing my possessions.

✝ 2. *Prosperity is mine. Divine health is mine. Peace and promotion is mine. I am protected from evil. In the name of Jesus Christ.*

---

3. *O LORD, You have saved me from the lion's mouth. You have delivered me from the wild ox. You have freed me from the devourer's cage. I shall stand and testify of your goodness before the congregation of your people. (Psalm 22:21-22)*

---

4. *"You are the LORD GOD ALMIGHTY. Your praise and glory fills the earth. Your praise fills my life. In Jesus name.*

---

5. *"I thank you, Lord, with all my heart; I sing praise*

to you before the gods. I face your holy Temple, bow down, and praise your name because of your constant love and faithfulness, because you have shown that your name and your commands are supreme. You answered me when I called to you; with your strength you strengthened me. **- Psalm 138:1-3.**

---

6. *"O Lord, even though you are so high above, you care for the lowly, and the proud cannot hide from you.*

---

7. ***"When I am surrounded by troubles, you keep me safe. You oppose my angry enemies and save me by your power.***

---

8. *"You will do everything you have promised; Lord, your love is eternal. You will complete the work that you have begun. In Jesus name.*

- Psalm 138:6-8.

THNAK YOU JESUS.

Part 3:

Violent Prayers for Healing, Business and Financial Breakthrough, and Freedom from Depression and Healing Of Anguish (Inner Hurts)

Chapter 10: 30 Violent Prayers for Healing

In this chapter, I have provided you with 30 powerful prayers for healing. These prayers are loaded with God's WORD to sack any sickness in your body.

1. PRAYER OF CONFESSION

1. Heavenly Father, I come to you in humility. Forgive me in every way I have lived in sin in the past. Forgive me from every kind of disobedience to YOUR WORD. In Jesus name.

---

2. According to your Word in 2Chronicles 7:14, I humble myself and confess my sins before you. LORD forgive me and heal my spirit, soul and body today in Jesus Name.

---

3. By the blood of Jesus, I receive forgiveness of sin and cleansing from all unrighteousness. Now I come to the throne of grace cleansed by the precious blood of Jesus. In Jesus Name.

---

4. I am sanctified by the Blood of Jesus Christ. I am healed by the Blood of Jesus. I overcome weakness and sickness of the body by the blood of Jesus. I overcome Satan and his demons by the Blood of Jesus.

2. DEALING WITH "UNFORGIVENESS"

5. O Lord, my Father, root out every seed of unforgivenes and bitterness in me, in the Mighty Name of Jesus.

---

6. I receive grace to forgive anyone who has offended me in the past. Henceforth, I hold nothing against anyone. I forgive everyone and receive my healing in Jesus name.

---

7. (Mention names) Lord, I release these ones who I have something against. I release them. Lord, forgive and bless them in Jesus name.

---

8. From today, I receive grace to walk in obedience, forgiveness and peace of mind. In Jesus name.

3. THE GRACE TO CARE FOR YOUR BODY

9. Heavenly Father, give me grace to take care of my body. I believe Your Word that my body is the temple of the Holy Spirit.

---

10. Every urge of carelessness, over eating, gluttony and love of food, die by fire in Jesus name.

---

11. From today, I receive the power to restrain and control myself on eating and drinking.

---

12. Food is made for man and not man for food. I have victory over my appetite. My eating and drinking will glorify God from today. I have control over my body, in the mighty of Jesus Christ.

4. AGAINST SPIRITUAL ATTACKS THAT CAUSE SICKNESS.

13. The bible says in Matthew 15:13 that 'Every plant, which my heavenly Father hath not planted, shall be rooted up'. Therefore, I root out every evil seed of sickness in my body right now, In Jesus name.

14. Every evil seed sower after my life, I bind and cast you into abyss right now, In Jesus name.

15. Whatever I have eaten, willingly or unwillingly, spiritually or physically, that is causing sickness in my body, be destroyed by fire right now, In Jesus name.

16. Any man or woman, spiritually or physically, projecting weakness, sickness, malaria, High Blood Pressure, etc, against me, perish by fire in Jesus name.

17. Every spirit responsible for this sickness (name it), I

dare you with God's Word. My body is the temple of the Holy Spirit. You have no right in my body and system. Therefore I command you to get out of this body and get down into abyss in Jesus name.

---

5. COMMAND YOUR HEALING.

18. It is written:

"But He was wounded for our transgressions, He was bruised for our iniquities; the chastisement of our peace was upon Him, and by His stripes we are healed." - **Isaiah 53:5.**

"Who his own self bare our sins in his own body on the tree that we, being dead to sins, should live unto righteousness: by whose stripes ye were healed" - **1 Peter 2:24.**

Christ has paid the ultimate price for my healing and divine health 2000 years ago. I have no reason being sick any more. Therefore I receive my healing right now, in Jesus name.

---

19. Heavenly Father, let Your healing power go through my veins and entire system right now. Let my body be healed and restored completely, In Jesus name.

---

20. I am healed. Yes. I am healed. I am healed. I am healed. I am healed. I am healed. I am permanently healed. In Jesus name.

---

6. MINISTER THE ANOINTING

21. (Anoint yourself and pray). By this anointing, I announce that my healing is sealed, in the heavens, on the earth, and under the earth.

22. Thank you Jesus for healing and setting me free. Glory is to your name.

...Thanks [be] unto God, which always causeth us to triumph in Christ, and maketh manifest the savour of his knowledge by us in every place.

- 2 Corinthians 2:14

How great is the goodness you have stored up for those who fear you. You lavish it on those who come to you for protection, blessing them before the watching world.

- Psalm 31:19

7. MINISTER THE COMMUNION

23.

O Lord, my Father. King of Kings and LORD of lords. As I take this communion, I am joined to the Body and Blood of Jesus Christ. Whatever cannot afflict Christ has no place in my system. In Jesus Name.

---

24. It is written in Ephesians 2:6 that I am raised up with Christ and seated with Him in the heavenly places, far above all principalities and powers, above sickness and diseases. In Jesus Name.

---

25. LORD Jesus, by eating your flesh and drinking Your Blood, I have eternal life working in me henceforth. (John 6:54). The life I live now is free from sorrows, sickness and disease.

8. THANK GOD FOR YOUR HEALING

26. O LORD my God, thank you for my healing. Your love and mercy has brought me total healing. May You be praised forever and ever. In Jesus name.

---

27. Lord, You have saved me from the lion's mouth. You have delivered me from the wild ox. You have freed me from the devourer's cage. I shall stand and testify of your goodness before the congregation of your people. (Psalm 22:21-22)

---

28. You are the LORD GOD ALMIGHTY. Your praise and glory fills the earth. Your praise fills my life. In Jesus name.

---

29. I thank you, Lord, with all my heart; I sing praise to you before the gods. I face your holy Temple, bow down, and praise your name because of your constant love and faithfulness, because you have shown that your name and your commands are supreme. You answered me when I called to you; with your strength you strengthened me. - **Psalm 138:1-3.**

---

30. O Lord, even though you are so high above, you care for the lowly, and the proud cannot hide from you.

When I am surrounded by troubles, you keep me safe. You oppose my angry enemies and save me by your power.

You will do everything you have promised; Lord, your love is eternal. You will Complete the work that you have begun. In Jesus name.

- **Psalm 138:6-8.**

Chapter 11: Violent Prayers for Business and Financial Breakthrough

God wants you to have financial abundance to be able to pay off your bills and have some left over. If the enemy is threatening your finances, you can pray violently and loose the angels of goodness and mercy to work and bring your supplies back to you.

However, there are a few key points I would like to state before we begin to pray and declare the promises of God over our finances.

1. Financial breakthrough does not mean that money will fall from the sky or that unknown persons will call you and give you huge sums of money for free or that you'll win lotto or football bet.

Someone messaged me the other day and asked me to go watch a video of manna falling from the sky. I said, "for real? Did you watch it?" He said yes and tried to persuade me. Unfortunately, I didn't get to watch the video.

Yes, I know that God can do all things, but it's not a good idea for us to expect manna to fall from the sky. That is, free food. The time we'll spend waiting for manna to fall from the sky and gathering it, we can invest such time in doing creative work and gather more manna from men.

There's also this misunderstanding in our faith churches. One or two persons shares a testimony of how someone called them after prayers and blesses them with money to solve their problems, then everyone claps and praises God. And consequently many believers starts praying and exercising faith that someone will call them and give them money too. Many now believe that if they haven't experienced that kind of miracle, that they've not gotten a financial miracle breakthrough.

That's a wrong mindset. First, I understand that occasionally God can ask people to call us and give us money and gifts. Sometimes such miracles happen to provide relief in serious crisis situations. But as Christians, we are not to live our lives hoping and expecting such occasional interventions as standards for provision.

2. Financial breakthrough means a new job with higher pay, a raise in salary, a new business idea or business connection.

The principal way that God blesses His people is through the works of their hands, that is, through your job or career or business. So if you don't have a job and you don't have a business, you can pray for God to give you a job or give you ideas to explore in starting your own business.

Apostle Paul said:

> *"For even when we were with you, we gave you this rule: "The one who is unwilling to work shall not eat." – I Thessalonians 3:10.*

The first thing is to have a willingness to work. Then back up that willingness by making sincere concerted efforts. Then we can pray and command God's blessings over what we are doing.

As we pray, God gives us ideas and shows us what to do, and connects us with the right people.

3. Financial breakthrough means divine direction over an investment or career or business decision.

In Genesis chapter 26, there was recession in the land. Isaac wanted to leave the country, but God appeared to him and told him to stay put and invest. He obeyed. The Bible then reports that, "Isaac planted crops in that land and the same year reaped a hundredfold, because the Lord blessed him. The man became rich, and his wealth continued to grow until he became very wealthy." (Genesis 26:12-13).

When there is a business opportunity or job opening before us, we don't just rush into it, no matter how spicy it smells. When things get difficult in our present career or business, we don't just run without looking back. As Christians we spend time and seek the LORD for direction on what to do. He may inspire us to go ahead with what we are doing or explore new doors or stay away. That way we'll be sure to get the best out of such jobs and businesses. That is part of what financial breakthrough is.

But also, don't expect everything to be easy because you're a Christian or because you spent 30 days fasting and praying or because you're sure God inspired you to take up the job or start the business or stay put in what you are doing and don't leave. Fasting and praying will clear off spiritual barriers and obstacles but you have to do some digging here and there.

Compare the case of Isaac. It's not easy planting crops when rain won't fall. Isaac had to work out a way to water his crops. He didn't hope that God would send rain on his farm because he heard from God to stay in the land or because he was a covenant child. He and his men dug a deep well; they sweated out the pain and took several days to dig in several places until they found water; and used the water to water their crops.

One thing about God's direction is that you're sure that as you work hard, you'll surely discover water to water your crops. You're working with hope and assurance that at the end you'll have reasons to smile.

4. Financial breakthrough also means pulling down strongholds of the enemy over your finances.

Sometimes the devil can attack your finances, like he did to Job. We may experience losses or extreme difficulty irrespective of how hard you work. When that is the case then you need to stand in God's Word and rebuke the devil.

If you're experiencing great financial challenges which are not as a result of laziness, you can stand in God's WORD and break the power of the devil over your finances. You can command the devil to loose his hold on your finances and release the angels of goodness to bring your finances to you.

Prayers for Financial Breakthrough

A. SCRIPTURES FOR CONFESSION

Luke 6:38 - Give, and it shall be given unto you; good measure, pressed down, and shaken together, and running over, shall men give into your bosom. For with the same measure that ye mete withal it shall be measured to you again.

Psalm 35:27 (KJV) - Let them shout for joy, and be glad, that favour my righteous cause: yea, let them say continually, Let the LORD be magnified, which hath pleasure in the prosperity of his servant.

Deuteronomy 8:18 - But thou shalt remember the LORD thy God: for [it is] he that giveth thee power to get wealth, that he may establish his covenant which he sware unto thy fathers, as [it is] this day.

Philippians 4:19 - But my God shall supply all your

need according to his riches in glory by Christ Jesus.

---

3 John 1:2 - Beloved, I wish above all things that thou mayest prosper and be in health, even as thy soul prospereth.

---

2 Corinthians 9:8 - And God [is] able to make all grace abound toward you; that ye, always having all sufficiency in all [things], may abound to every good work:

Psalms 1:3 - And he shall be like a tree planted by the rivers of water, that bringeth forth his fruit in his season; his leaf also shall not wither; and whatsoever he doeth shall prosper.

B. PRAYERS 1 – SUBMISSION

1. *"Heavenly Father, I give You praise because You delight in the prosperity of Your people. I give You praise because YOU supply my needs according to Your riches in Christ Jesus. Receive my praise today in Jesus name."*

---

2. *"How often do I think that prosperity, money and success is by my own efforts and volition alone. LORD, I come to YOU this day and confess my ignorance and pride. Forgive me for not giving YOU the ultimate place in my finances in the past. Forgive me and let Your mercy prevail over me this day, in Jesus name.*

---

3. *By the Blood of Jesus, I receive forgiveness of sins. I receive forgiveness from any form of greed and financial impropriety in the past. LORD Jesus let Your Blood speak for me spiritually from this moment, in Jesus name.*

4. "Thank YOU LORD Jesus because in YOU I have forgiveness of sins. In YOU I have grace to appear before the Almighty God to obtain mercy and find grace in time of need. In YOU I have assurance that when I pray, I receive answers. This is the confidence that I have, that as I pray for my finances this day, I have answers to Your Glory, in Jesus name.

C. PRAYERS 2 – GRACE TO OBEY

5. *"Almighty Father, as it is written in Your WORD, in Job 36:11, that if I obey and serve YOU, that I will spend my days in prosperity and my years in plenty. LORD, I come to YOU this day and ask for grace to obey YOUR Word on finances and in every aspect of life, in Jesus name.*

---

6. *"HOLY SPIRIT, I come to YOU today, I ask You to make me willing and obedient to the WORD of God henceforth according to Isaiah 1:19 so that I may eat the good things of the land. Uproot every seed of greed and disobedience from me this day, in Jesus name.*

---

7. *"Dear LORD, I ask YOU to make me a blessing in this world, that my life will be a light and support to those who are in need, for it is written that when I give, You will command men to give back to me. Inspire me to give and to give joyfully without regrets from today, in Jesus name.*

8. *"Holy Spirit, please motivate me and help me to honor the LORD with my resources and finances from this day, so that my barns will be full and overflowing with harvest, in Jesus name."*

D. PRAYERS 3 – REBUKE THE ENEMY

9. *"Heavenly Father, I stand in the authority in the name of Jesus Christ right now. I command every demon working against my business, my career and my finances to collapse, be bound and cast into the abyss, in Jesus name.*

10. *"It is written in Matthew 16:19 that whatsoever I bind here on earth is bound in heaven and whatsoever I loose here on earth is loosed in heaven. I therefore bind every spirit of poverty, lack, frustration and loss. I cast them into the abyss from today, in Jesus name.*

11. *"O LORD, based on Your Word we have authority here on this earth and according to (Mark 11:23) we can speak to the mountain and it will have to obey us. So devil, I speak to you in the name of Jesus Christ, I command you to take your hands off my finances right now in the Name of Jesus.*

12. "I speak to the mountain of Lack and Want, I command you to be removed and cast into the sea from this day, in the Name of Jesus.

---

13. "I hereby declare all curses against my life null, void, and destroyed from today. I am redeemed from the curse of poverty! I am free from oppression, in the name of Jesus Christ.

---

14. I now loose the abundance of God, and all that rightfully belongs to me now to start locating me, in Jesus name.

---

15. I thank You O LORD that You have a plan for me to overcome this have abundance. I cast all my cares and money worries over on You Lord. I WILL NOT WORRY anymore, neither will I FRET. I have peace and I'm enjoying God's supplies, in Jesus name.

16. *"It is written that angels are ministering spirits sent to minster unto the heirs of salvation. Therefore LORD, I ask that your angels of goodness, love and success begin to minister to my needs henceforth, in the name of Jesus Christ.*

---

17. *"Wherever my finances are, whoever is connected to my financial breakthroughs, O LORD, let your angels begin to reconnect them to me this day. As I step out to work on my business or career, LORD Jesus, men and women will bring me favor, in Jesus' name.*

E. PRAYERS 4 – THE POWER TO CREATE WEALTH.

17. *Heavenly Father, it is written that You give us power to create wealth. Therefore, I ask You to give me the power, wisdom and guidance to create wealth in my life. In Jesus name.*

---

18. *"LORD, I ask YOU today for ideas, I ask YOU for inspiration and divine strategies to turn my career around and grow my business into a global brand. Show me secrets hidden from men and help me to unleash YOUR full potential in what I am doing at the moment, in Jesus name.*

---

19. *"O LORD, make me an employer of labor, so that I will be a blessing to others and fulfill the covenant of Abraham which I inherit in Christ Jesus. Direct me to men and materials that YOU have assigned to bring me into my place of financial and business dominion before the world began, in Jesus name.*

20. *"Holy Spirit, You are my teacher. I ask You to teach me how to make profit in my business and career. Teach me to become a shining light in my business and career. Open my eyes to the right job opportunities and profitable business ventures, in Jesus name.*

F. PRAYERS 5 – COMMAND THE BLSSINGS

21. Heavenly Father, I thank YOU for Your Word, in Psalm 1:3, which says that I am like a tree planted by the riverside. Whatever I do prospers. Lord I pray, let your blessing and prosperity fill my house, in Jesus name.

---

22. "It is written in 1 Corinthians 9: 8 that God is able to make all grace abound toward me; that I, always having all sufficiency in all things, may abound to every good work.

"Therefore, LORD, I decree that from this day, I have all sufficiency in all things and I lack nothing. I decree that the grace of God is causing me to abound in every good work, in Jesus name.

---

23. "It is written in Psalm 112:3 that wealth and riches will be in my house, and his righteousness endures forever.

"So I decree that my house shall be filled with wealth

and riches in Jesus name"

---

24. "The Lord is my Shepherd. He prepares a table before me in the presence of my enemies. He anoints my head with oil. My cup runs over with blessings!

Money comes to me right now. God is opening the windows of heaven for me. He meets my every need according to His riches in glory by Jesus Christ.

He is causing men to give unto me good measure, pressed down, shaken together and running over, in Jesus name

---

25. God has given me the power to get wealth. I'm blessed in the field. I am blessed going in and going out. I have the favor of God. Favor, breakthrough, success, money and every good thing comes to me from this day, in Jesus name.

Chapter 12: 20 Powerful Prayers for Healing of Inner Wounds, Comfort and Freedom from Depression

We live in a world that is troubled on every side, because the devil, the adversary, has a mission to cause men to fear, lose their peace and perish with him.

Sometimes, we may be faced with situations that cause us to be troubled in mind, become sad, lose focus and worry about tomorrow. At such times, God brings us comfort in the Psalms. We can pray and be sure that God's power will restore us and keep us comforted.

Are you going through a situation that can only be described as sorrowful? A situation that only you fully understand the anguish that you are going through.

In this chapter, I am going to lead you to pray the Psalms and let God take over your anguish and bring you peace of heart. You'll be healed on the inside and your confidence will be restored.

PSALMS

Psalms 22:24 - For he has not despised or abhorred the affliction of the afflicted, and he has not hidden his face from him, but has heard, when he cried to him.

Psalms 56:8 - You have kept count of my tossings; put my tears in your bottle. Are they not in your book?

Psalms 116:1-2 - I love the LORD, because he has heard my voice and my pleas for mercy. Because he inclined his ear to me, therefore I will call on him as long as I live.

Psalms 46:1 - God is our refuge and strength, a very present help in trouble.

Psalms 55:22 - Cast your burden on the LORD, and he will sustain you; he will never permit the righteous to be moved.

Psalm 30:5: "For His anger is but for a moment, His favor is for life; weeping may endure for a night, but joy comes in the morning."

Psalm 147:3 - "He heals the brokenhearted and binds up their wounds."

Psalm 34:19 (NIV) - The righteous person may have many troubles, but the LORD delivers him from them all.

ADORATION

1. "Heavenly Father, I thank You for Your unending mercies towards me. Thank YOU for caring for me even when I don't know it. Your LOVE towards me is everlasting. I give You praise and honor forever and ever, in Jesus name.

---

2. "LORD, even when I'm hurt, YOU care for me. Even when I'm sad and grieved, YOUR love still protects me.

---

3. "You will not allow my soul to perish. Neither will You allow me to be comfortless. I praise YOU forever and ever, in Jesus name.

CONFESSION

4. "Heavenly Father, I confess that You have not despised and forgotten me.

No matter how grieved and sad I feel, I know that YOU still love me.

I know that YOU are working in my life and family to bring to pass YOUR eternal purpose.

I am confident in YOUR work in my life and family.

I rest in Your Love and promise, from now, to everlasting, in Jesus name.

SUPPLICATION

5. "LORD Jesus, I call upon you to be my comforter. Let YOUR Spirit comfort and strengthen my inner man.

"You are my present help in time of need. Heal my broken heart and wounds. Restore unto me the joy of salvation and confidence to proclaim my faith before the world.

---

6. "I cast my burden on YOU, O LORD, sustain me and do not allow my faith and spirit to be moved, in Jesus name.

---

7. "LORD Jesus Christ, I believe and confess that YOU have delivered me from all my troubles. You have taken away my heaviness of heart and given me joy and confidence. Yes, I have joy; I have faith in the LORD. I have confidence and victory at all times, in Jesus name.

---

8. "Holy Spirit, guide me in this situation to respond to

people and issues appropriately. I accept You as my comforter. I am comforted by YOU. In Jesus name.

---

9. "O LORD, I will bless YOU at all times: YOUR praise shall continually be in my mouth. My soul shall make her boast in thee, O LORD. Grant me deliverance LORD, that all men shall hear thereof, and be glad.

---

10. "LORD, I seek YOU this day, hear me, and deliver me from all my fears and hopelessness.

---

11. "Lighten my soul for I look unto THEE. Deliver me from misery, hopelessness and depression. Take away my heaviness and shame from me, in Jesus name.

---

12. "LORD, deliver me from all my troubles for I trust only in YOU. Restore my Joy of salvation and cause Your blessings to reign in my life and household. In Jesus name.

13. "Even though the young lions do lack, and suffer hunger, because I seek and serve YOU, LORD, cause me not to lack any good thing. My mouth shall be filled with testimony and I shall declare Your goodness before the brethren, in Jesus name.

---

14. "LORD, I thank You because Your eyes are upon me and Your ears are open to my prayers. Let all those who cause my troubles and pains be visited by Your mighty power from today, in Jesus name.

---

16. "Thank YOU LORD for delivering me from all my afflictions. Thank YOU LORD for keeping my bones and soul from being broken. Thank YOU LORD for redeeming my soul from satan, through the Blood of Jesus Christ.

---

17. "I decree that it is well with my spirit, soul and body, in Jesus name.

18. *Satan, I rebuke you. Whatever seed of depression you have sown in my heart is hereby uprooted in Jesus name.*

---

19. *I decree that I receive the joy of the LORD and my heart is healed and full of praise to the LORD. The joy of the LORD is my strength at all times. In Jesus name.*

---

20. *"I claim my victory over depression, fear, worry and anxiety. From this day forward, I refuse to be afraid and worry anymore. For the LORD cares for me. He will not let even the very hairs of my head to touch the ground. He will always provide for me. I am safe and secure at all times, in Jesus name.*

Chapter 13: 5 Ways to Maintain Your Victory, Healing and Deliverance

Getting delivered is great. Getting healed is wonderful. But keeping your healing and deliverance permanent is best. Jesus said:

"When the unclean spirit has gone out of a person, it passes through waterless places seeking rest, but finds none.

Then it says, 'I will return to my house from which I came.' And when it comes, it finds the house empty, swept, and put in order.

Then it goes and brings with it seven other spirits more evil than itself, and they enter and dwell there, and the last state of that person is worse than the first. So also will it be with this evil generation." – **Matt. 12:43-45**

Jesus is simply saying here that there is a probability that one gets delivered from sickness, curses and evil spirit attacks and the problems come back again and the situation become worse than it were in the beginning.

But it doesn't have to be so.

The Word of God gives us an idea of how we can keep our deliverance and victory permanent.

1. DO NOT KEEP YOUR SPIRIT EMPTY.

From Jesus' statement above, it's evident that if you leave your spirit empty, you might get attacked with a worse situation.

Consequently, it's essential to fill your spirit with positive thoughts and vibrations. Fill your mind with God's Word on a daily basis.

> *"Keep this Book of the Law always on your lips; meditate on it day and night, so that you may be careful to do everything written in it. Then you will be prosperous and successful. - **Joshua 1:8."***

Work out a system to read the Bible daily, one or two chapters a day and your spirit will have content that will resist the enemy at all times.

2. SERVE THE LORD

*"So you shall serve the LORD your God, and He will bless your bread and your water. And I will take sickness away from the midst of you. No one shall suffer miscarriage or be barren in your land; I will fulfill the number of your days." - **Exodus 23:25-26:***

Find a place in God's kingdom and do His work. Join in sharing tracts, the prayer team, the ushering department... just get busy for the LORD, and no enemy will have grounds over your life.

3. EXERCISE YOUR FAITH.

It is possible that you experience some form of attack, temptation, and setback in your life, from time to time. That doesn't necessarily mean that you're not delivered or that the sickness didn't go.

It's crucial for you to believe that you have been delivered and confess your deliverance, and stop running to and fro looking for other types of prayers for deliverance anymore. Remember what the Bible says:

> *"Now faith is the assurance (title deed, confirmation) of things hoped for (divinely guaranteed), and the evidence of things not seen [the conviction of their reality—faith comprehends as fact what cannot be experienced by the physical senses]. 2 For by this [kind of] faith the [a]men of old gained [divine] approval* - **Hebrews 11:1(AMP).**

4. SHARE YOUR TESTIMONY

When you share your story with others, your blessings become permanent. Jesus told the healed man...

" Return to your home, and declare how much God has done for you." And he went away, proclaiming throughout the whole city how much Jesus had done for him - **Luke 8:39 (ESV)**

5. LEARN TO MAINTAIN A POSITIVE OUTLOOK ABOUT LIFE AND KEEP SPEAKING POSITIVE THINGS ABOUT YOUR LIFE

Proverbs 18:21 - Death and life [are] in the power of the tongue: and they that love it shall eat the fruit thereof.

1 Peter 3:10 - For he that will love life, and see good days, let him refrain his tongue from evil, and his lips that they speak no guile:

Ephesians 4:29 - Let no corrupt communication proceed out of your mouth, but that which is good to the use of edifying, that it may minister grace unto the hearers.

God

Bless

You

Other Books by the Same Author

1. Prayer Retreat: 21 Days Devotional With Over 500 Prayers & Declarations to Destroy Stubborn Demonic Problems.

2. HEALING PRAYERS & CONFESSIONS

3. Violent Prayers for Deliverance, Healing, and Financial Breakthrough.

4. Hearing God's Voice in Painful Moments

5. Healing Prayers - Prophetic Prayers that Brings Healing

6. Healing WORDS: Daily Confessions & Declarations to Activate Your Healing.

7. Prayers That Break Curses and Spells and Release Favors and Breakthroughs.

8. 120 Powerful Night Prayers That Will Change Your Life Forever.

9. How to Pray for Your Children Everyday

10. How to Pray for Your Family

11. Daily Prayer Guide

12. Make Him Respect You: 31 Very Important Relationship Advice for Women to Make their Men Respect them.

13. How to Cast Out Demons from Your Home, Office & Property

14. Praying Through the Book of Psalms

15. The Students' Prayer Book

16. How to Pray and Receive Financial Miracle

17. Powerful Prayers to Destroy Witchcraft Attacks.

18. Deliverance from Marine Spirits

19. Deliverance From Python Spirit

20. Anger Management God's Way

21. How God Speaks to You

22. Deliverance of the Mind

23. 20 Commonly Asked Questions About Demons

24. Praying the Promises of God

25. When God Is Silent! What to Do When Prayer Seems Unanswered or Delayed

26. I SHALL NOT DIE: Prayers to Overcome the Spirit and Fear of Death.

27. Praise Warfare

28. Prayers to Find a Godly Spouse

Get in Touch

We love testimonies. We love to hear what God is doing around the world as people draw close to Him in prayer. Please share your story with us.

Also, please consider giving this book a review on Amazon and checking out our other titles at www.amazon.com/author/danielokpara.

I also invite you to check out our website at www.BetterLifeWorld.org and consider joining our newsletter, which we send out once in a while with great tips, testimonies, and revelations from God's Word for victorious living.

Feel free to drop us your prayer request. We will join faith with you, and God's power will be released in your life and the issue in question.

About the Author

Daniel Chika Okpara is a husband, father, pastor, businessman and lecturer. He has authored over 50 life-transforming books on business, prayer, relationship and victorious living.

He is the president of Better Life World Outreach Centre -www.betterlifeworld.org - a non-denominational evangelism ministry committed to global prayer revival and evangelism.

He is a Computer Engineer by training and holds a Master's Degree in Theology from Cornerstone Christian University. He is and is married to Prophetess Doris Okpara, his prayer warrior, best friend and biggest support in life. They are blessed with two lovely kids

NOTES

Made in the USA
Coppell, TX
15 September 2020

38063553R00104